STAINED GLASS PRIMER

VOLUME 2

advanced skills & : annotated bibliography

by
PETER MOLLICA

photography by
CHARLES FRIZZELL

mollica stained glass press

1940-A BONITA AVENUE • BERKELEY, CALIFORNIA 94704 • (415) 849-1591

To Maestro Rufo
and this time to
Judy and Jennie

Table of Contents

INTRODUCTION

The techniques covered by this book are an extension of the basic skills as taught in **STAINED GLASS PRIMER Volume 1.** . They are more advanced techniques for the student who has done some panels and feels secure in the basics and wants to add to his or her knowledge of the medium.

The methods described have worked well for me and are adapted for the artist working alone on a fairly small scale. Large studios may have developed variations that work well in shops of 5 to 50 craftspeople. The methods described are based upon the traditional training that I have had in-studio and from books. I feel that there is no substitute for in-studio experience, but some people prefer to learn from a book at their own pace.

I think books can be helpful, especially after a basic level of craftsmanship has been reached. I have included in this volume an extensive annotated bibliography.

Chapter 1
BUILDING AND USING
A PLATE GLASS EASEL

Introduction

In this chapter I will describe the method which I have found to be the simplest and most direct for building and using a small plate glass easel. Such an easel is a desirable device when cutting glass for leaded glass panels, since it enables you to wax up pieces of stained glass to judge their color with daylight coming through them.

The easel itself is simply a piece of 3/16" or 1/4" thick plate glass, which is set in front of a window.

Traditionally a window facing north is chosen, since it gives an even, indirect light all day for most of the year. Any window will work but, if direct sunlight hits your easel, the wax which is holding your stained glass in place will soften and let your pieces fall. This makes a south light least desirable; an eastern light less desirable in the morning, and a western light less desirable in the afternoon.

An east or west facing window has an advantage. Since an east or west facing easel gives you a variety of light conditions, you can choose your cutting time to approximate the light conditions your stained glass panel will receive when finally installed. That way you can get a better idea of how it will eventually look.

However, when using your easel in direct sunlight you must be aware that the sun is melting your wax and watch closely for slipping pieces. You will need to block the sun when you are not actually using the easel. An opaque window shade or piece of cardboard can be used for this purpose.

Fig. 1 A small window, *courtesy Lynn Barretti.*

Fig. 2 Determining the size of an easel.

A frame to hold your plate glass can be made from 2" x 3" pieces of wood. Smaller size wood can be used if your plate is small. It is important that your frame be solid so that it doesn't wobble while you are trying to use it.

Used plate glass is just as effective as new and has the advantage of costing less. It may be scratched or dirty and may need to have irregular edges trimmed to make the corners square. However, most glass shops will be glad to square up the piece of glass they sell you. If your plate is large it is worth having the glass shop deliver it after you have built your frame. You can have them place it right on your frame and then you will not have to manage doing so alone.

Determining the Size of Your Easel:

If the window in front of which you have chosen to build your easel is small, for example, only 18" x 36", you can still have a larger easel space, perhaps as large as 40" x 70", by following this method. (Fig. 1)

Buy a roll of white tracing paper 40" wide at an art or drafting supply store. Measure from floor to ceiling and cut off a piece of tracing paper that length. Tape one end of it to the ceiling two feet in front of the window. You will see that the paper diffuses the light fairly evenly and enlarges your light source considerably. You can then determine how large an easel your window will light. (Fig. 2) You may want to hang this paper behind your easel while cutting out your stained glass.

Fig. 3 Uprights in position

Fig. 4 Placement of uprights.

Building Your Easel:

For the sake of illustration, let's say that you have chosen to make your plate 32" x 60". You will need two straight 2" x 3" uprights, tall enough to lean against the wall above the window and yet be about 18" from the wall at the bottom. The 2" side of the 2" x 3" should touch the wall at the top. (Fig. 3)

Cut the bottom end of these 2" x 3" uprights at a slight angle so that they rest flat on the floor when leaned against the wall as described. (Fig. 4)

Fig. 5 Secure cross pieces to uprights.

Fig. 6 Secure shelf piece to uprights.

Cut two pieces of 2″ x 3″ each 30″ long. On the 30″ pieces of 2″ x 3″ mark the center of the 2″ side on each end. If the bottom of your plate is to be about 18″ from the floor, measure from the bottom ends of your uprights and make a mark at the 18″ point. Lay the uprights on the floor and line up the center marks on one 30″ piece with the 18″ marks on the uprights. Nail or screw the pieces together. (Fig. 5) Measure up 60″ on each upright and make a mark. Line up the center marks on the second 30″ crosspiece with the new marks on the upright and nail or screw them as before.

Cut a third 30″ piece of 2″ x 3″. Lay this piece across the uprights just below the 18″ mark. Nail, screw or bolt this piece in place as shown. It will act as the shelf on which the plate will rest. (Fig. 6)

This frame can now be made secure by nailing it to the floor at the bottom and the wall at the top. It is now ready to accept your 32″ x 60″ plate glass easel. (Fig. 7)

Fig. 7   Completed easel.

14

Fig. 8 Easel with tracing paper behind.

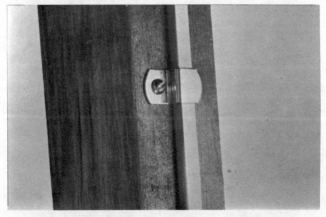

Fig. 9 Mirror clips holding plate to frame.

If you measured accurately, the uprights should support the long edges of your plate and the crosspieces should support the shorter edges. "Mirror clips" or wooden blocks should secure the top of the plate to the frame. (Fig. 8) and (Fig. 9)

You may decide that you don't want a permanent easel, or one so large. Perhaps you only need a 20" x 30" piece of plate which can simply be propped up on a window sill. (Fig. 10)

Fig. 10 Simplest easel, *courtesy Brenda Hunt.*

16

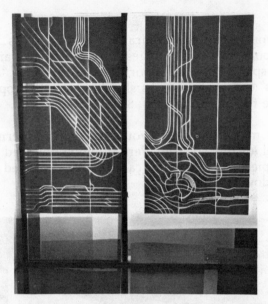

Fig. 11 Patterns in place on easel with tracing paper behind.

Fig. 12 Remove tracing paper frequently.

Using a Plate Glass Easel:

You can cut out your entire stained glass panel, then wax (See Chapter 2 for easel wax recipe) the pieces up on the easel, change the pieces you don't like, then take them all down and glaze them. This is a quick method in common use, but I don't like it as well as the following:

Make your cartoon and cut out the patterns using pattern shears. Tape your cartoon to the back of the plate. Stick the patterns to the front of the plate using the cartoon as a guide. Soften a small piece of the easel wax by working it with your fingers. When it is soft, roll a ball of it about the size of a pea. Place this ball of wax in the center of the back of a pattern and stick the pattern in its proper place on the easel. Use the cartoon as a guide and leave about 1/16" between the patterns.

When all of the patterns are in place, remove the cartoon and hang a large piece of tracing paper behind the easel. (Fig. 11)

In addition to giving you a large area of diffused light, the tracing paper also eliminates distractions such as trees, buildings, etc., which may be outside your window. It is easier to work this way since you will be able to judge colors and color intensities more accurately without being fooled by a tree.

A tree behind your piece of pale blue glass can make it dark and greenish.

However, you will want to remove the tracing paper frequently to see how the glass looks without it. There is always quite a difference, especially if you are using transparent "antique" glass. (Fig. 12)

Fig. 13 Applying easel wax to glass.

Also, you must constantly keep in mind what distractions will exist outside the panel when it is finally installed. When measuring the opening for which you will be making a stained glass window, make a sketch or photograph of what is seen through the opening. This will be of great help later when you are choosing colors.

For example, if the roof of the building overhangs so that the top 12" of your stained glass window will always be in shadow, you will need to be aware that that section is going to look darker and you will probably need to use lighter glass in that portion. A dark color that looks fine in the center of such a window might go almost black up top.

The movement of trees outside your stained glass can really make it come alive, especially if you use transparent "antique" glass. However, they can also work against your design if you do not take them into consideration when choosing your glass.

A deep luminous panel of dark ruby glass can look beautiful on your easel but go black when installed in a window that faces a grove of trees which you forgot was there.

Now that you have built and positioned the easel and have mounted your cartoon and pattern pieces to your satisfaction, you are ready to begin cutting the glass pieces.

Choose a pattern, cut the glass to fit it and place a small lump of wax in three or four places along the edge of your piece. (Fig. 13) Press it into place on the easel by pressing only at the places where there is wax. (Fig. 14)

Fig. 14 Sticking glass to the easel with wax.

Next remove another pattern. You will want to hold the sheet of glass up to the light where the pattern was to better judge if you have chosen the right color. If you are satisfied, cut the piece and wax it up in place. Using this method you can judge the color next to the pieces you have already chosen, or find the exact part of a sheet that will look best. This careful selection process is an important part of designing a small stained glass panel.

When your pieces are all cut and waxed up on your easel you can change the pieces you don't like and study the finished selection. Perhaps you'll want to go behind your easel and paint in the lead lines using lampblack for an even closer approximation of what your window will look like when completed.

Fig. 15 A rack for trays built into a glazing bench.

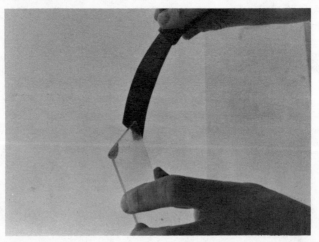

Fig. 16 Using a putty knife to release the wax from the easel.

Trays

When you are satisfied, remove the glass from the
easel and arrange it in wooden trays ready for glazing.
If your studio is small you may see no need for trays as
you can conveniently remove the pieces from the
easel one at a time as you need them. However, if your
glazing bench is not near your easel or you are going
to paint on your glass you will need trays to lay your
glass out on. They are simple to build, and a
convenient rack can be built to store them (full or
empty) under your glazing bench. (Fig. 15) If you have
room, you should make them about 24" x 36". Smaller
ones will do, but any larger will be cumbersome to
carry. The bottom can be made from masonite,
particle board, or thin plywood. The particle board is
the cheapest and works well. The edge can be 1" x 1"
wood molding nailed around the rim. If you do not
have room for many trays you can make one with a
deeper edge and stack your glass in layers with
newspaper to separate the layers.

Fig. 17 Removing easel wax from glass.

Fig. 18 Remove glass from easel and arrange in trays.

Care should be taken when removing the glass from the easel. While holding the piece in place with your left hand, slide a putty knife or razor blade scraper under the wax which will release it from the easel and allow you to lift the glass off without prying (which could chip the glass). (Fig. 16) Remove excess wax from the piece (Fig. 17) and place it, in order, in your tray. (Fig. 18) When all the pieces are removed, clean the easel by scraping off and saving the pieces of wax and then cleaning the plate with acetone or paint thinner to remove the spots left by the wax.

These solvents will leave a film which can be cleaned off with weak ammonia or Windex.

Fig. 18-a & 18-b Completed window set up on easel for final inspection and cleaning.

From Connick, ADVENTURES IN LIGHT AND COLOR.

26

Fig. 19 Supplies for making easel wax.

Chapter 2
MAKING EASEL WAX

Introduction

There are many ways to stick your pieces of stained glass to your plate glass easel. You'll need to try several to decide which works best for you. I've tried every one I've come across but I keep returning to the one I was first taught to use. It requires a bit of alchemy, but I think it is worth the effort. I'll describe how to make it and then discuss some of the alternatives.

You'll need: (Fig. 19)
Beeswax, from art store or candle makers' supply
Cornstarch, from grocery store
Olive oil or salad oil, from grocery store
Rosin, from violin store or sporting goods store
Double boiler with lid
Hotplate
Pie pan
Measuring spoons

Recipe for Easel Wax

4 oz. (2" x 2" x 1½") Pure Beeswax
5 Tablespoons Cornstarch
1 Tablespoon Olive Oil
½ teaspoon Powdered Rosin

28

Fig. 20 Break wax into small pieces for easier melting.

Fig. 21 Sprinkling corn starch.

A piece of beeswax 2" x 2" x 1½" weighs about 4 oz.

Melt a piece this size in a double boiler. It will melt faster if you break it up into small pieces. (Fig. 20) Boil water in the bottom pan and melt your wax in the top pan. It is important to use a double boiler since wax is very flammable. Buy an inexpensive one since it will only be good for melting wax when you are finished.

When the wax has melted, add five level tablespoons of cornstarch. (Fig. 21) Sprinkle the cornstarch in a little at a time, since it causes the mixture to foam up. Stir until the cornstarch has dissolved, and all lumps are gone. The cornstarch helps make the beeswax more workable.

Add one tablespoon of olive oil or salad oil. This helps to make the wax less crumbly.

Finally, add ½ teaspoon of powdered rosin. This helps the wax harden up a little when it is pressed onto the easel. In warmer climates you might find that a little extra rosin will keep the wax from softening too easily.

Fig. 22 Pour out a sample for testing.

Fig. 23 Once hardened, the wax can be softened in your hands.

When your ingredients have all melted and are mixed, pour a small sample of your mixture onto an oiled pie pan and allow it to cool. (Fig. 22) The cool wax should be fairly hard, but should soften easily when worked for a moment with your fingers. If it is too soft it will not hold your larger pieces of glass and if too hard will be difficult to work with. You can test it by using it to stick a large size piece of glass to your easel. Three to six blobs of wax around the edge of the piece should hold it to your easel indefinitely. If it works well, pour the rest of the mixture into the pan and let it cool. (Fig. 23)

Your new batch of easel wax will stick to your hands a bit. If you collect the used wax off your glass and easel carefully, so that it doesn't pick up splinters of glass, you can re-use it on your next window. The more times it is used, the better it becomes. The dust and dirt that it picks up seem to make it stick less to your hands and improve its workability.

Although variations on this wax formula have been used by stained glass studios for generations, it is still far from perfect. You may find that a particular batch holds the glass up but will not hold your patterns up as well, or vice versa. Do not expect perfection from this mixture. It is, however, better than the alternatives that I have tried.

32

Fig. 24 *Art Wax*, a good easel wax.

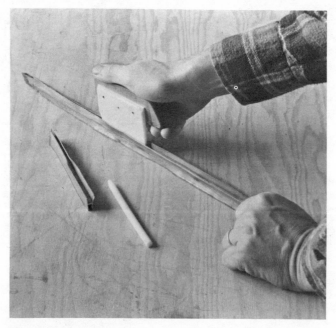

Fig. 25 *Teflon* as a lead opener.

Alternatives

PLASTICENE is all right, but a bit soft, and much too greasy. It doesn't hold large pieces well and the glass must be carefully cleaned so that the grease does not get transferred to the lead while glazing, which would make it impossible to solder.

3M or FORD MOTOR CO. "STRIP CAULK" is better than Plasticene since it is not greasy, but it is still soft and doesn't hold large pieces well.

HOT PURE BEESWAX can be dripped onto the corners of the glass as it lays on the horizontal easel plate. It hardens up and holds the glass very securely, but has the inconvenience of having to be done with the easel laying flat on the bench, making changing of pieces a bit more time consuming. However, many large studios use this method exclusvely and wouldn't change.

"ART WAX" or "BULLETIN BOARD WAX" (Fig. 24)

I have only recently been introduced to this wax. It is used by graphic designers and is available in art stores. It is too soon to be sure, but this product may be just as good as the kind you mix from beeswax. So far it has performed very well, but only prolonged use will tell if it will replace the home made stuff. It is good to remain open to innovations. *Just as "Teflon" makes a far better lead opener than a wooden lathekin, perhaps "Artwax" will replace beeswax.* (Fig. 25)

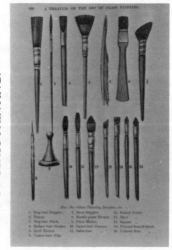

From Suffling, A TREATISE ON THE ART OF GLASS PAINTING.

Chapter 3
GLASS PAINTING &
SURFACE ABRADING TECHNIQUES

Introduction (Glass Painting)*

Painting with a black pigment on glass has been part of the technique of stained glass since at least the 7th Century. The earliest fragments of ancient stained glass work in western Europe have black paint fired into them. The black paint was used to delineate facial features, drapery folds and similar details on the pieces of colored glass.

Modern styles of abstract design have used it to heighten the painterly quality of the window, adding spontaneous gestures of paint—similar to paint application in some abstract expressionist painting. Paint can also be silkscreened onto the glass using all the varied effects obtainable with the silkscreen process.

Glass painting can be a very complicated subject. Methods of mixing and using stained glass paint vary dramatically from one painter to the next. I will introduce you to the basic tools and skills which you will need to get started. Should you decide that glass painting is your bag, I would refer you to "Making Stained Glass" by Robert Metcalf, and "Technique of Stained Glass" by Patrick Reyntiens, which describe various painting techniques.

*Glass painting supplies mentioned in this chapter are available from: L. Reusche & Co., 2-6 Lister Ave., Newark, New Jersey 07105, as well as some stained glass suppliers.

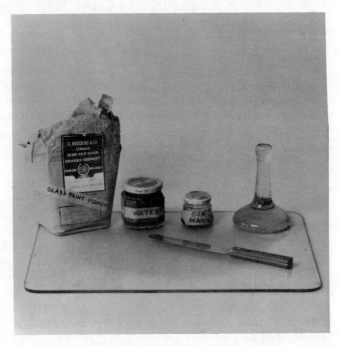

Fig. 26 Glass paint, water, gum arabic, a glass muller, palette knife, glass palette.

Preparation of the Paint

Glass paint is made from brown or black metal oxide with powdered glass added to make it fuse in the kiln. It comes in powdered form and must be mixed with a liquid medium and ground smooth before use. Every conceivable medium has been used for mixing glass paint, from wine or molasses to hundreds of different oils. We will use water.

You will need a piece of plate glass about 16" x 16" to use as a palette on which to mix and grind the pigment. You will also need a large palette knife, a glass muller, some gum arabic and a jar of water. (Fig. 26)

I use #1051A, Deep Black. I find that it remains opaque when fired, and so lessens the necessity of repainting. Reusche offers a number of other black and brown pigments, i.e., tracing black, tracing brown, ancient brown, bistre brown, etc. You may wish to experiment with different paints or mixtures of paints. Many studios use a mixture of brown and black in some proportion which they have found to be to their liking. They are all prepared in the same way.

Fig. 27 A pile of pigment.

Fig. 28 Add water a little at a time.

In the middle of your 16" x 16" palette, make a 1" high pile of pigment. (Fig. 27) Make a depression in the top of the pile, like the mouth of a volcano. Into this depression pour a small amount of water and push the pile of pigment in on top of it, a little at a time. (Fig. 28) Use your palette knife to mix the water and the pigment together, trying to keep the water from running off the pile of pigment. When all the pigment is wet (you may need to add more water as you mix), begin grinding it with the palette knife. You will find with some practice you can become adept at grinding the paint in a circular motion and moving it all back into a compact pile. To grind it use the knife flat, crush the pigment against the glass palette and move the knife in a circle against the palette. (Fig. 29) This spreads the paint out in an ever widening circle and if done long enough will eventually grind the paint pigment to a fine creamy mixture. Turn your knife over occasionally to grind the paint that accumulates on top of it.

Fig. 29 A circular motion with the palette knife grinds the pigment.

To speed up the process, use a glass muller. (Fig. 30) You will still use a circular motion and the action of the two glass surfaces will grind the pigment fine. When the paint is spread out so that it almost covers the palette, you should use your palette knife to move it back into a neat pile and start over again.

The action used to pile up the paint is tricky and you'll find that it takes some practice before you can clean up your palette without leaving trails of paint leading to your paint pile. Making a pile of your paint will keep it from drying out, so it is worth learning this tricky skill.

Fig. 30 A glass muller speeds up the grinding.

Hold your knife with your thumb placed on the back of the blade as shown. (Fig. 31) Lift the leading edge (the edge furthest from you) of your knife about ½" off the palette and leave the trailing edge firmly pressed to the palette. Now push the knife across the palette away from you using your thumb for pressure. Let the trailing edge of the knife push some paint across the palette to your future pile. The knife should carry the paint leaving the palette scraped clean behind it. (Fig. 32) When you get to where you wish to drop the paint, stop the forward motion of the knife and lower the leading edge of the blade and firmly press the knife flat to squeeze the paint from beneath it. With the knife still pressed glat, slide it back from the pile of paint, this should leave all the paint in the pile and now your knife should be fairly clean (Fig. 33) and ready to repeat the scrape and squeeze process until all your paint is pushed back into a neat pile and the rest of your palette is clean. (Fig. 34) *It is a joy to watch this being done by a master.*

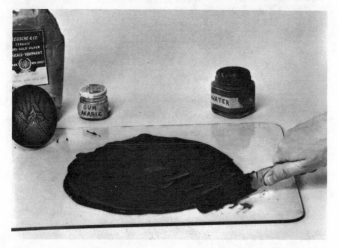

Fig. 31 To make a paint pile: Holding the knife.

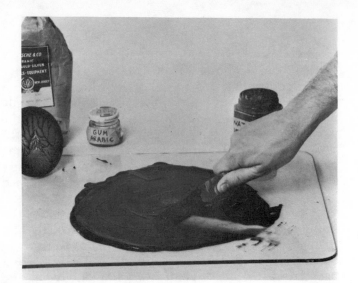

Fig. 32 Pushing the paint.

Fig. 33 Leaving the paint in a pile.

Fig. 34 A paint pile.

The amount of grinding time required will vary depending on how hard you press and how long your arm holds out. Some masters insist that the paint be ground smooth and left covered overnight, then ground smooth again before use. In studios doing a lot of painting, the painter will simply make it a rule to replenish and re-grind his paint supply each evening before quitting.

The true test is in the firing. If you are not grinding your paint enough the particles will not blend as well in the fire and your paint, which was opaque when you put it in the kiln, will become transparent where the particles did not blend. If this happens, you can paint over the original paint and re-fire it, but it is wiser to grind enough the first time.

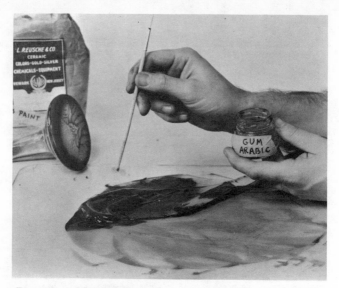

Fig. 35 Adding gum arabic.

Fig. 36 *Frying:* paint on the left has *fried* in the kiln.

If your paint is ground enough you will notice a significant decrease in the size of the pigment particles. Spread the paint thin with your palette knife and look closely at it before you start grinding. You will be able to see the wet particles about the size of fine sand. When you finish grinding the particles should be almost invisible in the creamy mixture of paint. If you cover your paint pile with a glass bowl or similar dish, you can leave it for some time without fearing that it will dry out. You can grind for ten minutes, then cover it and go to lunch and grind some more, then cover it and sweep up the shop, then grind, etc., etc.

When you paint on your glass, the water will evaporate leaving the paint pigment as a residue on the glass. If you add a drop or two of gum arabic solution to your paint, while grinding, it will stick tighter to the glass and not be so likely to be accidentally smudged. (Fig. 35) If you add too much gum arabic, the paint will dry hard and brittle and chip off when you try to scratch your name in it with a sharp stick. Make this sharp stick test before using the paint. The stick should scratch a sharp line in the paint with no chipping or fuzzy edges. Paint that is too hard will be difficult to control and too much gum arabic will cause the paint to "fry" in the kiln. "Frying" is when the paint bubbles and burns away in tiny pin-holes, requiring re-painting (Fig. 36)

If your paint is well prepared, you are ready to start painting.

The two traditional glass painting techniques are *tracing* and *matting*. Countless modern variations on these techniques are also used, including dripping the paint or applying it with a sponge, silk-screening or air brushing it on. Perhaps you'll think of some new methods.

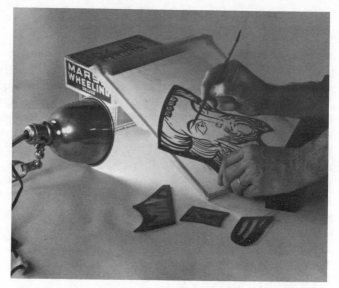

Fig. 37 The simplest light box arrangement.

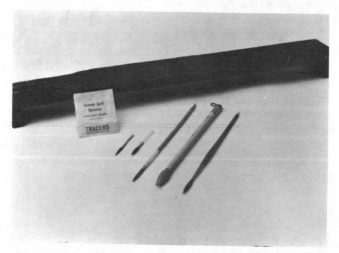

Fig. 38 French quill *tracers*, Chinese brush, sable *rigger*.

Tracing

The heavy, dark, usually opaque, black lines painted on stained glass windows to add detail, such as facial features and drapery folds, etc., are traced from the original cartoon onto the glass. Occasionally, this type of painting is done free-hand while the glass is stuck up on the easel, but usually it is done by laying the glass on the cartoon and tracing. A simple *light box* is very handy for tracing, expecially when the glass is dark. (Fig. 37) The brush used for tracing can be either: *1" oxhair or sable rigger, 1" camel hair tracer mounted in a quill,* or a *Chinese calligraphy brush.* (Fig. 38) The Chinese brushes may be the easiest and cheapest to locate, although Reusche sells the others. Whichever brush you use, the hairs should be long and pointed and springy.

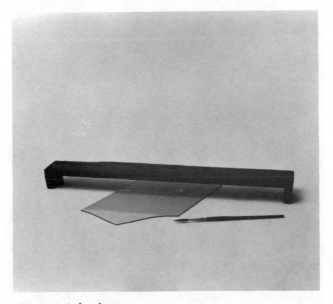

Fig. 39 A bridge.

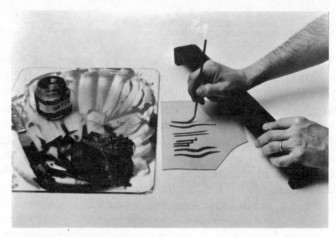

Fig. 40 Tracing practice.

Fig. 41 Filling the tracer.

The other important tracing tool is called a *bridge*, and it is a ½" x 2" x 16" piece of wood with 1¼" blocks of wood at each end to make a bridge over your piece of glass. (Fig. 39) It is used to rest the heel of your hand on while tracing. It allows your fingers to act as freely as they do when you rest the heel of your hand on your pad of paper as you write. Since the paint is easily smudged and your hand will get grease on the glass, it would be folly to let your hand rest on the glass and it is difficult and tiring to paint or write freely without resting the heel of your hand. The bridge may seem awkward at first, but it is worth the effort as it will help you to develop your skill as a tracer to the fullest.

Practice making long smooth strokes with your hand resting on the bridge. (Fig. 40) Work with it until you can control the thickness of the line and end each line in a graceful point. Refill your brush constantly, keeping it full of paint that is wet enough so that the brush hairs do not show in the paint on the glass. Be sure that the brush is full of paint so that you can make a whole stroke without stopping to re-fill your brush.

Begin by wetting the brush in water, then fan the hairs of the brush out against the palette and, picking up plenty of paint, roll the hairs of the brush into a point. This will assure that the brush is loaded completely. (Fig. 41) Fill in each line so that it is opaque and no brush strokes show. If you are not using a light box, hold your piece up to a bright light frequently to be sure it's opaque. The paint strokes can be filled in or added to as long as the paint is wet. If wet paint is added over dry paint, the two layers will not fire correctly in the kiln and "frying" will result. (see Fig. 36) So, keep your paint wet enough to work with at a relaxed rate. (It is better to use fluorescent lights in your light box, since bulbs heat up the box and dry your paint too rapidly.)

50

Fig. 42 15th century painted head, *courtesy Victoria & Albert Museum.*

Fig. 43 Pencil study by John-Auguste-Diminque Ingres, 1863. *Courtesy National Gallery of Canada.*

Learning to paint heads in a medieval style can be valuable if it is heads you are interested in. (Fig. 42) The bold line and simple detailing is one of the most effective techniques for painting heads on glass. Later styles, like the renaissance and the pre-raphaelites, painted a more realistic head (Fig. 43) with subtle tracing and very fine shading. Admirable technique, but much of its effect is lost when placed in a window against strong sunlight.

The distance from which the head will be viewed has much to do with the way it should be painted. In large windows where the figure is to be seen from some distance, the painter will use thicker, simpler lines, since the subtle delicate line will be "washed out" by the strong light.

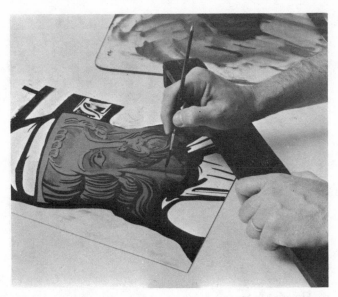

Fig. 44 Tracing a face.

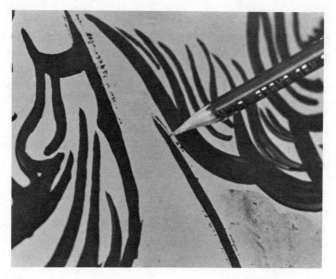

Fig. 45 Using a stick to clean up tracing.

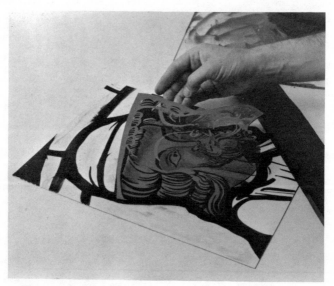

Fig. 46 A traced face.

To Trace A Face:

Place your *clean* glass over the cartoon, making sure it is accurately cut and positioned. *(To clean the glass you can use a little of the paint mixture smeared on the glass and wiped clean with a cloth or tissue. This will remove the dust or grease which would make painting difficult.)* Put your bridge so that you can conveniently rest your hand and trace the lines of your cartoon onto the glass. (Fig. 44) Do as accurate and neat a job as you can. If you make a drastic error, simply wipe the piece clean with a damp cloth and begin again. But if the lines are just a bit messy, let the piece dry and clean them up with a sharp stick. (Fig. 45) Be careful to clean off any excess particles of pigment so that it doesn't become a permanent part of your glass when fired.

When the piece is finished, place it in a tray and go on to the next piece. Be sure that dust does not accumulate on your painted pieces, since it will cause the paint to "fry" in the kiln. (Fig. 46)

When your tracing is complete, or you have enough pieces to fill your kiln, fire them. (See Chapter 4: Kilns and Firing) After they are fired and have cooled, you will want to re-wax your window onto your easel for inspection and possible matting. Any incorrect tracing should be re-painted and re-fired at this time.

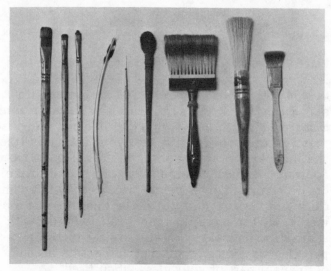

Fig. 47 3 scrubs, a quill, a needle, a mop, a badger, hog-hair stippler, camel hair duster.

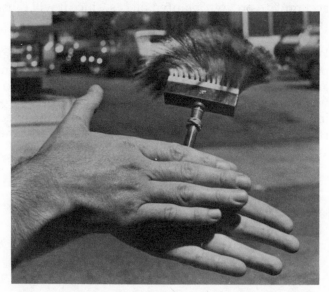

Fig. 48 Drying my badger.

Matting

Matting is applying a thin layer of paint to the glass and, when it is dry, stippling and brushing away some of the paint to create highlights and other shading and modelling effects.

For this process you will need a collection of odd brushes for different effects: cut-off oil painting brushes (called scrubs, skews, stipplers), a "mop" for applying the wet paint (camel hair is best, but any soft, long hair brush will do), and a "badger blender" for spreading the paint evenly over the glass while it is still wet and for some "stippling" effects. (Fig. 47)

The "badger blender" is very important in traditional glass painting. The master glass painter protects his "badger" with his very life. English or German badgers are so called because the bristle is badger hair, chosen for its propensity to have split ends. A good badger hair produces a thin, almost invisible stroke and it is the only thing that seems to spread the paint smoothly and evenly in a thin layer over the entire piece of glass. It is not used for applying the paint, but for spreading it out evenly. It must be kept clean to do its job, so must be washed and dried frequently.

Badger

Washing a Badger:

Rinsing in water is enough if done regularly. A badger should be dry before use. Drying a badger is a ritual that is often cursed as tedious and time consuming, but is necessary to prolong its useful life. If the round handle is rolled back and forth between the palms of your hands, the hairs will spread and throw off much of the water, much the same method a live badger would use to dry himself. (Fig. 48) This spinning in the air will dry the brush in a minute or two. Some painters slap the hairs back and forth against a wooden bench leg. This drives out the water quickly. (Fig. 49)

Fig. 49 Slapping excess water from a badger.

Matting a Face

The face that has been traced and fired should be
wiped clean of dirt and grease and waxed up on the
easel. A layer of matt is painted on with the "mop"
brush (Fig. 50) and smoothed with the badger
blender.

Fig. 50 Using a *mop* to apply matt.

Fig. 51 Badgering a face.

Fig. 52 Using the badger to stipple the paint after blending.

The blender is held delicately as one might hold a cup of tea. The blender is held at right angles to the surface of the glass and stroked gently across the surface of the glass with a very light touch. (Fig. 51) Start to the left of the face, brush across the face letting only the very tips of the badger hairs touch the surface and continue on past the right edge of the face. Now go back across the face from right to left, then left to right again and so on until the matt has been evenly spread over the whole surface of the face. (Fig. 52) If your matt was applied fairly evenly to begin with, you will be surprised how effective the badger will be. (Fig. 53)

At this stage, the painter begins to work the paint towards the desired texture.

Fig. 53 Blending effect of the badger brush.

Fig. 54 Using a mahlstick, *courtesy Designex Studio.*

Fig. 55 Stippling effect of the badger brush.

When painting or working matt with the glass waxed up on the easel you cannot use your bridge easily, so instead a sign painter's MAHLSTICK *is used. One end rests on the easel, the other end is held in your left hand about 6" from the easel. Your right hand with the brush can rest conveniently somewhere in the middle, just as it did on the bridge. (Fig. 54) A piece of round broom handle with some friction tape on the end makes a crude, but functional mahlstick.*

While the paint is wet you may use the badger to "stipple" the paint, that is, still holding the badger at right angles to the surface of the glass, stab directly downward so that each hair makes a little hole in the wet matt surface. Done while the paint is wet this leaves an evenly mottled looking surface, and helps in evenly distributing the paint. (Fig. 55) If done when the paint is dry, called dry stippling, the holes are sharply defined and the effect is called a "stippled" surface. Dry stippling may be done with the badger or with a *hog hair stippler* (Fig. 56) whose bristles are white and stiff and produce a sharp, distinct stippled effect.

Whether you wish a blended, mottled or stippled effect is entirely up to you. Most glass painters begin a face by blending and wet stippling with the badger and then dry stippling with the hog hair stippler.

Fig. 56 Dry stippling with the hog hair stippler.

Fig. 57 Ancient painted head, notice highlights on nose, lips, eyes, & hair.

You now have an even layer of paint over the entire surface of the face and it is time to decide where the strongest highlights will be. This depends on how the face is lit. Choose a direction from which you would like the light to come and imagine which parts of your face would be in the most light and which in the most shadow, and which in between. Usually the forehead, the ridge of the nose, the cheek bones and the lower lip will get the most light, and the eye sockets, area beneath the cheek bones and area just beneath the lower lip will get the deepest shadow.

The spots where the light hits the strongest are called highlights (Fig. 57) and all or almost all of the matt is removed at these points using a stick, stiff scrub or even your finger. (Fig. 58) and (Fig. 59) The areas around the highlights will fade off to shadow and this can be acheived by stippling or brushing some of the paint away. (Fig. 60) Areas that are in shadow are stippled very lightly or not at all. In this manner the face can be gradually made to look as real as is desired. The glass painter who desires a realistic looking effect will switch from his stippler to a needle with which he removes tiny particles of paint at a time, gradually achieving the effect he desires. (Fig. 61) A tight little squiggly motion of the needle all over the surface will remove all traces of brush strokes and leave texture quite similar to the lines and pores that make up the texture of our skin. (Fig. 62) *Look at photographs of various styles of painted heads and try duplicating the ones you like.*

Fig. 58 Taking out highlights with a scrub.

Fig. 59 Taking out highlights with a stick.

Fig. 60 Removing paint from light areas of face.

65

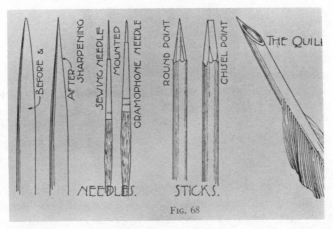

Fig. 61 Needles, sticks and quills.

Fig. 62 Using needle to texture paint.

Often the painter will use two or three or more separate matts, firing between matts to get his desired effect. From the first matt he will remove the paint completely from all but the most shadowed areas. Subsequent matts will add the middle tones and make the shadows darker and eventually even the highlights may have a layer of matt over them. In this way, the painter can control the effect of the face even in the strongest sunlight.

If a face receives strong sunlight, it will need more paint so that the shading will show up. In weak sunlight, such as northern windows or under an overhang, the painter may leave the highlights bare and paint only lightly.

Light works similarly on the folds of drapery or the planes of buildings, so if you will be doing much representational painting on glass, it will be essential that you look closely at your friends, your clothes, and your house.

Fig. 63 Thayer & Chandler Airbrush, Model E, *courtesy George McKeever Studio.*

If your use of paint will be non-representational and more expressionistic, you will use an infinite number of methods for applying and removing the paint till you get just the effect you desire. You can drip, spatter, brush, roll, smear, sponge, etc. to your heart's delight. *See: Techniques of Stained Glass by Patrick Reyntiens, for examples of expressionistic painting effects.*

Airbrush

Glass paint can also be silkscreened or airbrushed. The entire process of applying and badgering the paint to produce an even matt can be done in one operation with an artist's airbrush. (Fig. 63) Some of the shading and stippling effects described can also be achieved with an airbrush and a skilled hand.

Not many glasspainters use airbrushes, yet, but I think it is stubbornness. The airbrush does lend itself to easy rendering of realistic effects (as in the paintings of some of the Hyper-Realists). The traditional glass painters, today, want to stay away from such realism. It may be because the accepted historical view sees the advent of painterly realism in 16th century stained glass as the beginning of decline for the medium. They warn against the repeating of that decadence. Warnings or no, I think we will see an increased use of the airbrush techniques in stained glass.

If you decide to try it, you should consult the manufacturer to determine what size you will need. The one picture in Fig. 63 is made by the Thayer & Chandler Co. of Chicago. It is a model "E" and it works with glass paint if the paint is filtered through fine cloth after it is ground. If not filtered it will clog the nozzle.

68

Fig. 64 Example of stick lighting by Lisbeth Hoffman.

© Verlag J. Hannesschläger, Augsburg.

Stick-lighting

Another very useful painting technique is called "stick-lighting". You used it a bit in scratching out highlights while painting the ancient head. Traditionally it was used for inscriptions which were very common in early windows. It also allows the use of freer drawing techniques as in this figure by Lisbeth Hofmann. (Fig. 64)

I will explain a traditional method for stick-lighting an inscription on glass. Cut the glass to the required size, then lay on a dark matt of paint and badger it smooth. (Fig. 65) Do a full-size drawing of your inscription. (Fig. 66) Place the drawing on the glass and trace the letters. (Fig. 67) Your pencil will scratch away the outline in the paint through the paper. (Fig. 68) (*If your paint is very hard, you can rub chalk on the back of your drawing before tracing and the chalk will be transferred to the glass.*) (Fig. 69) You can then carefully scratch away the paint within the outlines using a sharp stick or stiff scrub. (Fig. 70)

You can also work directly on the matt and not bother with the drawing. This allows for more spontaneous effects. Some artists sign their windows using this technique. Experiment using bone, a goose or turkey quill or your finger for different effects. (Fig. 71)

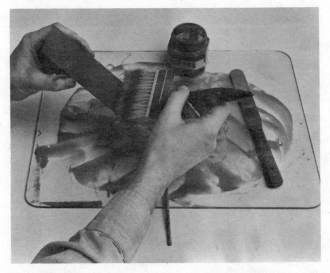

Fig. 65 Smoothing paint before stick lighting.

Fig. 66 Do a drawing.

Fig. 67 Trace onto glass.

Fig. 68 Tracing shows on paint.

Fig. 69 Chalking drawing back.

Fig. 70 Scratching out an inscription.

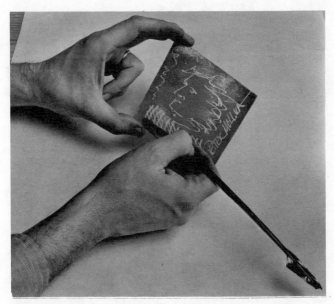

Fig. 71 Spontaneous stick lighting with a quill.

Fig. 72 Applying silver stain to the back of painted glass.

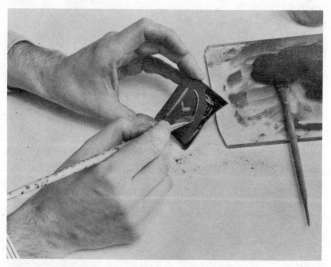

Fig. 73 Removing dry stain with scrub.

Silver Stain

In 1425 it was discovered that silver when fired into glass turned it yellow.

Reusche & Co. sells silver stain which will fire to a light yellow, and others for dark yellow or orange. It is expensive and there are a few tricks to successful staining.

The pigment is mixed with water in the same way you mixed your black or brown paint. However, a special palette and palette knife should be used since the silver stain is very corrosive. *All tools should be cleaned immediately after use.*

Apply a thin layer of stain to the *back* of the piece of glass you wish to stain, so that it does not interfere with any paint which may be on the front. (Fig. 72) Badger the stain till it is evenly spread over the surface of the glass. When it has dried to a brownish residue, any excess may be removed with a scrub or stick. In this way you can be very accurate about where you apply stain. (Fig. 73)

Silver stain fires at a lower temperature than paint and is usually fired separately. Stain can sometimes be fired in the same firing with paint if the stain is fired face-down on the kiln tray.

Tests should be run in your kiln to determine the right length of time to fire stain. If it is fired too long it will "metal". "Metalling" is the formation of a metallic coating over the stain leaving it mottled and dark. If fired correctly, the brownish residue will look about the same after firing, but when rubbed away reveals the transparent yellow stain on the glass.

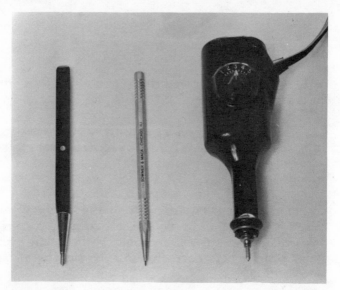

Fig. 74 Diamond scribe, carbide scribe, electric carbide scribe.

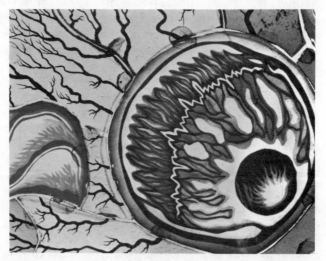

Fig. 75 Example of acid etching, *courtesy of D. Fenton*.

Introduction (Surface Abrading)

In ancient windows, the glazier would sometimes abrade or scratch off the flash layer of his glass leaving the base color exposed. Most often this was done to flashed ruby on white so that the ruby glass would have clear areas showing through. If you try this, you'll appreciate what a difficult task it is, even with modern carbide scribing tools. (Fig. 74)

Some time later it was discovered that Hydrofluoric Acid would rapidly eat away the flash. The glass is masked with wax or asphaltum varnish or "Con-Tact" paper and immersed in the acid until the unmasked areas of the flash are eaten away. (Fig. 75)

Hydrofluoric Acid is still used by some studios, but the acid and its fumes are extremely dangerous and should be used only under laboratory ventilating hoods by people aware of the hazards. Etching pastes, or etching frosts, are mixtures of hydrofluoric acid and ammonium fluoride. They act the same as hydrofluoric acid alone, but take longer. They are readily sold in supply stores, but still very dangerous and I don't recommend their use.

Better results can be obtained by the methods of wheel engraving and sand-blasting.

Fig. 76 Variable speed stone lathe, *courtesy A. Magdanz, CCAC.*

Fig. 77 Engraving wheels.

Wheel Engraving

Scratching the surface of glass by hand, using a carbide or diamond scribe, produces a white abraded effect. Small electric tools with carbide or diamond tips do the same thing, but do it faster. Today professional engravers use a variable speed stone lathe. (Fig. 76) On the shaft of this lathe can be mounted various size and shape wheels. The wheels are made of natural sandstone or, more commonly today, aluminum oxide or silicon carbide. (Fig. 77) An expert engraver shapes his stones (called "dressing the stone"), to achieve whatever type of cut is required.

Above the wheel a drip-hose allows water to constantly flow onto the stone as it turns. The water cleans the stone and most importantly cools the glass. Without the water, the friction of the wheel on the glass would cause great heat and the glass would crack. For very accurate, fine engraving, copper wheels in combination with silicon carbide powder and oil are substituted for the stone wheels and water.

The engraver begins with a coarse stone at a fast speed to get a rough cut and then, by varying the speed or switching to finer grit smoothing stones, he finishes the cut and makes the outlines accurate and smooth. (Fig. 78)

Fig. 78 Engraving with stone lathe.

Fig. 79 Polishing with cork wheel and pumice.

Fig. 80 Example of engraved and polished glass.

The engraved area now has a frosted look. If transparency is desired, the engraver switches to a wooden or cork polishing wheel. These wheels do not do the polishing, but act as a vehicle for the pumice powder or jeweler's rouge which will do the actual polishing. (Fig. 79) If optical quality is required a felt wheel in combination with cerium oxide powder is used for a final polishing. (Fig. 80)

Fig. 81 Air compressor.

Fig. 82 Pressure pot.

Sand-Blasting

Sand-Blasting is done by masking off all areas that don't require abrading and subjecting the glass to a pressurized jet of sand or silicon carbide particles. The glass not masked will be frosted or deeply carved by the abrasive depending on how long and at what pressure the glass is subjected to the jet. It is also possible to cut all the way through the glass if desired.

The equipment consists of an air compressor, pressure pot, hose with various size nozzle jets, a sealed cabinet, and an air cleaning system. (Figs. 81-84) Self-contained units which include all of these, except the compressor, in a metal cabinet are available. They do limit the size of work you can do to the size of the cabinet. (Fig. 85)

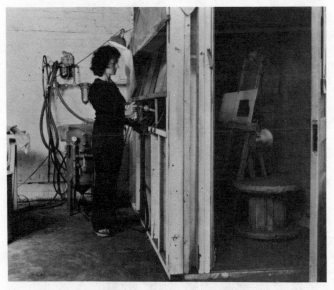

Fig. 83 Blaster points nozzle through rubber curtain into blasting cabinet.

Fig. 84 Air cleaning system, cabinet contains filters.

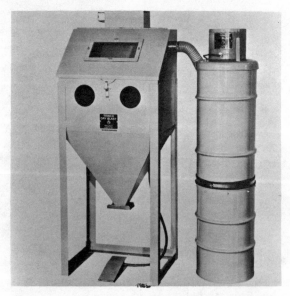

Fig. 85 Self-contained sand blasting, *courtesy Trinity Tool Co.*

Either system is very expensive and, at least for your first projects, you will want to locate a firm in your area that does sand-blasting and hire them to do yours. You can buy abrasion resistant tape to mask areas which you don't want blasted. As a substitute, two or three layers of ordinary masking tape will work. Sometimes "Con-Tact" paper is used, but is not as reliable. The edges tend to lift up, causing fuzziness.

Fig. 86 Detailed masking using abrasion resistant tape.

Fig. 87 Using sharp knife to cut out areas to be exposed.

For detailed blasting (Fig. 86) you can cover the entire piece with masking and use a sharp knife or razor blade to cut out and peel away the areas you wish blasted. (Fig. 87) Make sure your masking is firmly stuck to the glass, especially around the edges where you have cut out your design. The piece is now ready to be placed in the blasting cabinet (Fig. 88) and subjected to the abrasive. (Fig. 89) The result will have a frosted appearance. (Fig. 90) and (Fig. 91) It is possible to polish this surface back to clear using a cork polishing wheel and water and pumice powder— the same as polishing an engraved piece.

Fig. 88 Placing the glass on the easel in the blasting cabinet.

Fig. 89 Blasting, *courtesy Ann McAndrew.*

Fig. 90 The resulting frosted area.

Fig. 91 Detail of work by Beverly Reiser, the white areas are frosted.

Carving

With varying pressures or exposure times it is possible to produce various depths of carving with the sand-blaster. The resulting shadows produce a sculptured surface which can be very effective. (Fig. 92)

Fig. 92 Example of various depths of sand blasting, circa 1920, *courtesy N. Fogel.*

Mask the entire piece. Cut away the mask from the area you wish to be carved deepest. Blast the exposed area.

Now cut away the area you wish to be carved medium deep. Blast the whole piece again.

Now cut away the area you wish to be only frosted. Blast the entire piece again.

By this successive method of cutting away mask and blasting you have subjected the first area you cut away to three blasts and this area will therefore be the most deeply carved. The second area you cut away got blasted twice and the third area you cut away got only one blast.

Fig. 93 Gas fired glass stainers kiln, *courtesy Designex Studio.*

Chapter 4
KILNS AND FIRING

Introduction

Almost any type of kiln can be used to fire glass paint. I will discuss three which work especially well.

The best I have used is the gas kiln with jets that spread the flame out above a single large tray. (Fig. 93) These are sold as *glass stainers kilns* or *flash kilns* by L. Reusche & Co. for about $2000. They are well worth the investment for large studios.

However, many large studios use an electric kiln big enough to fire several trays at once. These trays are stacked an inch or two apart. Because heat rises, the glass on the top trays tends to fire quicker than the glass on the lower trays. This necessitates firing the kiln slowly so that the temperature rises fairly evenly throughout the chamber.

Installing a small circulating fan in this type of kiln will make it fire much more evenly. The fan circulates the heated air so it does not settle at the top. Figures 94 and 95 show such a kiln with a fan installed in the back wall. Even with the fan, however, this type of large electric kiln will need to be brought up to temperature more slowly than the smaller kiln discussed below.

Fig. 94 Elecric kiln with Marinite XL trays and circulating fan. *Courtesy George McKeever Studio.*

The best trays for a kiln are made from ½" *Marinite XL,* a fireproof material developed by Johns-Manville Company for use as bulkheads on ships. It is made to withstand continuous exposure to temperatures of 1200 degrees F., so it is excellent as a tray for firing glass paint. The glass to be fired can be placed directly on the tray without fear of distortion or sticking while being fired. Marinite XL comes in 4' x 8' sheets and can be cut with a saw to convenient sizes for kiln trays. Small pieces of Marinite XL can be stacked up to make legs to hold up the next tray. (Fig. 94)

When Marinite XL is new it is gray; when it has been fired many times or fired above 1200° F., it may become reddish. New trays of Marinite XL should be fired for three or four hours with the kiln door left open to drive out moisture and gases which could cause the Marinite XL to warp or crack. Once they have been *cured* in this manner they will last indefinitely.

For a studio doing large amounts of glass painting, the flash kiln or large electric kiln is a necessity. If you are planning only an occasional painted window you'll find it more practical to borrow *kiln-time* from a potter or purchase an inexpensive, small, electric potters' kiln. (Fig. 96)

Fig. 95 Installation of fan in back of electric kiln.

Firing Glass in a Small Electric Kiln

Usually the chamber of small kilns is at least 12″ deep so that three or four trays can be stacked in them. If Marinite XL trays are not available, you can use the ceramic trays the potter uses. *Ceramic trays take much longer to heat up slowing down your firing time.*

Fig. 96 Small electric kiln.

Fig. 97 Sprinkling kiln wash to glass won't stick to ceramic tray.

Glass will stick to bare ceramic trays so *kiln wash* or *plaster of Paris* should be sprinkled on each tray before the glass is placed on it. (Fig.97) Press the pieces of glass into the sprinkled plaster so that it will compress into a smooth surface beneath the glass allowing no room for air bubbles to form. Place all the glass on the tray with the painted side up. (Fig. 98) None of the pieces should touch each other or the sides of the kiln, since they might stick together.

Fig. 98 Glass in kiln, painted side up.

For pottery the kiln must heat up very slowly to as high as 2200° F., but for glass paint it need only reach 1200 ° to 1400° F. and can be brought up to that temperature quite rapidly. The kiln pictured here (Fig. 96) reaches 1200° F. in 45 minutes. In a small kiln this will not cause major problems of uneven firing as it would in a larger kiln. If the glass on the top trays tends to fire more quickly than the glass on the bottom trays, you can correct for this by loading the harder glasses (usually reds, oranges and yellows) on the top trays and the softer glasses (usually blues, greens, purples and tints) on the bottom trays. If this does not correct the problem, you will have to go back to slower firings. Kilns and glasses vary so much that most of your firing knowledge will come from experience with your own particular kiln.

Visual Check of Fire

Your kiln should have peep holes in the top or sides (with stoppers made of fire brick) (See Fig. 96) so that you can check to see if the glass is fired. When you have used the kiln a few times, you will know approximately how long it takes to fire your glass but firing times will vary slightly with the size of the load or the weather conditions, so you must check visually. Subsequent firings will be shorter as the kiln will be already partially heated up.

The coils of the electric kiln glow and light up the inside of the kiln so that, when it is on, the whole inside looks orangy-red. To check your glass you must switch off the kiln. Look in the peep hole. You will see it start to get darker inside and then the plaster and glass will have a darker, redder glow. If the glass is *not* fired, it will look blackish against the glowing plaster. When it *is* fired, the glass and the plaster will both glow equally with an intense, dark, hazy red color. The paint will then have merged with the surface of the glass and, when cooled, will be shiny like the glass. As the critical time approaches, the kiln should be checked frequently. If fired too long the glass will begin to distort and flow. If the edges of the glass have become rounded and fire polished, the glass was fired too long and will probably have shrunk slightly during cooling.

Using Cones to Check Fire

Instead of visual inspection to check your firing, you may rather use *Pyrometric Cones*. They are small pyramids of clay which you stand upright in your kiln. They are made so that they bend at pre-determined temperatures. For glass paint a cone #020 works about right. When you think your kiln should be just about done, you peek in through a peephole at the cone and, if it has started to bend over, your firing temperature has been reached and you can turn off the kiln and let it cool. With some trial and error, you will be able to determine the correct number cone for your firing temperature.

Unloading the Kiln

When you have determined that your glass is fired, close the peephole and leave the kiln off for ten minutes. Then open or slide back the top an inch or two (called *cracking the kiln*) (Fig. 99) for another ten minutes. Then open it halfway for five minutes before opening the top completely. The glass is still too hot to remove and should be allowed a few more minutes to cool in the kiln. For top loading kilns and for flash kilns the pieces of glass are lifted from the tray with a trowel bent as in Figure 100. The trowel is preheated by resting it on the edge of the kiln (Fig. 99) or imbedding it in the hot plaster on a tray. *A cold metal trowel will cause the hot glass to crack.* The glass is lifted from the kiln and placed in your wooden trays to cool.

This procedure is about the fastest that the kiln can be emptied. If you are firing only one batch of glass you can just switch off the kiln and let it cool while closed. This will take several hours. Some kilnmen recommend a much slower cooling than I have described, but, with the small kiln, I have not encountered any problems with this sequence. The glass can be cut after firing, if desired, and I've had no instances of cracking. Very thick pieces should be cooled longer before removing from the kiln.

Fig. 99 Preheating trowel in *cracked* kiln.

Fig. 100 Using trowel to remove glass from kiln.

The firing of glass in small kilns is not as difficult nor critical as it is sometimes made to sound, so do not hesitate to try it with whatever kiln facilities you can locate.

Your painted and fired pieces should be waxed up on your easel again to check their final appearance. It is easier to correct any flaws in painting now before it is leaded up.

98

Fig. 101 Bulging window has broken away from its saddle bars. *Courtesy Margo Marsh.*

Chapter 5
REINFORCING & INSTALLING STAINED GLASS

REINFORCING STAINED GLASS

Introduction and Theory

A stained glass panel requires some strengthening to keep it from sagging under its own weight. The bottom pieces of glass are, after all, carrying the weight of the glass and lead of the whole panel. Lead, being a very soft metal, will not be able to support the glass over a long period of time. The glass expands in hot weather and may stretch the leads. In cold weather the glass contracts, but the lead contracts less and therefore stays stretched. These slight movements season after season will eventually dislodge particles of hardened waterproofing cement from between the glass and lead and weaken the window. The window will begin to bulge and leak and perhaps lose pieces. (Fig. 101)

Reinforcing will not solve this problem entirely, but it can help the window to resist sagging due to wind and pressure changes. This is most noticeable in churches where the window openings are large and numerous. Keeping the large naves of churches heated requires that the doors seal nearly airtight. It is a theory that the action of closing the large doors of a church will cause slight momentary increases in air pressure on the inside of the building. This slight pressure outwards and the buffeting by the wind cause the minute movements which slowly weaken a stained glass window. Reinforcing does lessen this movement and can help prolong a window's life.

100

Fig. 102 Stiffening bar soldered to panel and notched into wooden frame.

Fig. 103 Notched frame for stiffening bar.

If well made and well installed, a window may go as long as 50 or 60 years without needing attention, although it should be inspected for sagging or weakening cement every 5 or 10 years. I have seen windows which have not been re-glazed in more than 100 years, but this is really much too long. The lead will have deteriorated badly by then and the cement will have fallen out, making the window very fragile.

There are two types of reinforcing in general use: the "stiffening bar" which is soldered directly to the leads of the panel, and the more traditional "saddle bar" which is installed in the frame of the window opening. The window is then tied to the saddle bar with wires.

If your panel is to be installed as a window you should design for reinforcing bars every one or two feet. The position of the re-bars is critical to the design of your window as well as to its support. Determine how many re-bars your panel will have and where they will go before you begin designing.

Stiffening Bars

After repairing many old windows, I have come to the conclusion that the stiffening bar is the better form of reinforcing. (Fig. 102) The kind of support it gives is suited to the kinds of stresses which plague a leaded window. It seems logical, too, that if the ends can be secured to the frame, it is desirable to have the stiffening bars run vertically. This would decrease the likelihood of bulging. This is not always practical and no reinforcing bar seems to be totally effective.

I've noticed that in practice, most craftsmen reinforce their windows as much as they can in a manner which has the least detrimental effect on the aesthetics of the window design.

Fig. 104 Stiffening bar cut to fit under metal frame.

Fig. 105 Soldering stiffening bar to panel.

The stiffening bar is usually a flat brass or galvanized steel bar ⅛" x ⅜" soldered on its edge to the lead joints of the panel. The galvanized steel is harder to solder and the availability of darkening solutions at stained glass supply stores makes the brass a better choice, even though it's more expensive.

The reinforcing bar is usually on the inside surface so that it is not exposed to the weather and does not cast a shadow on the window. When the window is installed in a wood frame, the wood can be notched to fit the ends of the bars. (Fig. 103) In stone or metal the end of the bar can be cut to fit neatly between the window and the frame without taking up too much space. (Fig. 104)

The flat stiffening bar can be bent to follow the path of the lead so that is is not visible in the finished window. Bent bars are not considered to be as strong as straight bars running directly across from one edge of the frame to the other. Straight bars are, of course, shorter and therefore less flexible. I think the difference is negligible.

Other methods of stiffening are: soldering a stiff wire along the leads or even just coating the leads with solder over their entire length.

Soldering Stiffening Bars

When your panel is complete, including cementing and cleaning, cut your flat stiffening bar to length. If it is going into a wooden frame, make it long enough so that each end can be notched into the frame. If it is going into a metal frame, cut the end as shown (Fig. 104), so that it can slip behind the frame.

Clean the bar for soldering; sand paper works well. A strong flux, such as Dunton's "tinners fluid" works best, but the oleic acid or LA-CO flux you use to solder your leads will work well on brass.

Lay your bar in place on your panel and solder it securely wherever it crosses a soldered joint. (Fig. 105) It is a good idea to design your lead lines so that several jonts line up with your bar so that it can be strongly attached. If soldered to a single lead, instead of at an intersection, it will not be as strong.

When your bar is securely soldered, wipe off all the excess flux and use a bit of whiting and a scrub brush to remove all grease and dirt. Your panel is now ready for installation.

Saddle Bars

"Saddle bars" are usually ⅜" round steel bars. They are installed in the window frame before the stained glass is installed. (Fig. 106) In wood frames, a deep hole (1¼") is drilled into one side of the frame, and a shallow hole (½") at the same height on the opposite side of the frame. (Figs. 107 and 108) The bar is cut to length 1" longer than "daylite size" so that one end can be inserted in the deel hole and the other end slipped into the shallow hole. (Fig. 109)

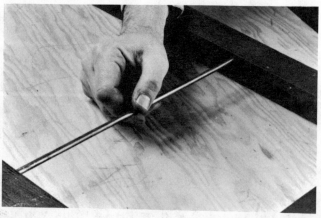

Fig. 106 Saddle bars are installed in the frame before the window is installed.

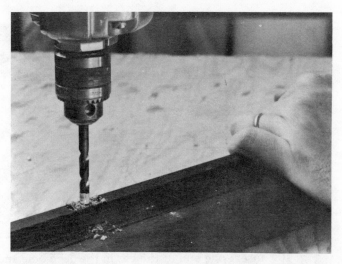

Fig. 107 Drill a deep hole (1¼″) in one side of the frame.

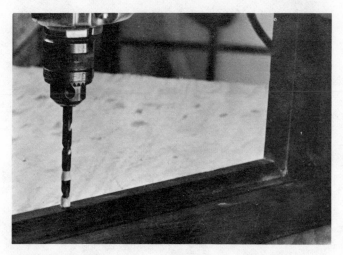

Fig. 108 Drill a shallow hole (½″) opposite it.

Fig. 109 Insert one end of the bar in the deep hole and slip the other end into the shallow hole.

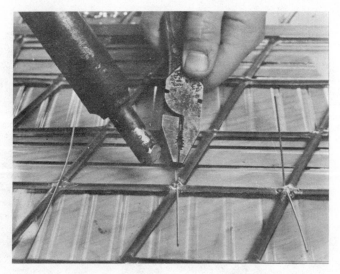

Fig. 111 Soldering *banding* wires to panel.

The window is then installed and tied to this bar with copper wires. (Fig. 110)

Soldering Saddle Bar Wires: (called Banding)

You must design your panel so that several intersection joints of your leadline lie along the proposed path of the saddle bar. To these joints you can solder 6″ lengths of #14 or #16 copper wire so that they are attached in the center with the two ends free. (Fig. 111) These wires will be wrapped around the saddle bars during installation and the ends twisted tightly together.

Your panel is ready to be installed.

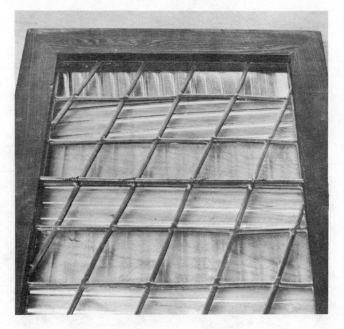

Fig. 110 Saddle bar installed and panel wired to it.

Fig. 112 Hammer, hacking knife, putty chisel, linoleum knife, propane torch.

Fig. 113 Using putty chisel.

INSTALLATION

Introduction

Installing leaded windows can be very enjoyable, especially if the weather is fair. It is very satisfying to see a window installed that you've worked hard on.

Installing will involve the use of carpentry and metal working skills, as well as the skills of the putty glazier. In general, it is best to allow plenty of time, since installations always seem to take much longer than you estimate. Unforeseeable problems arise which may require trips to the hardware store, lumber yard and (sad as it is) back to the shop to repair a cracked piece. However, that's all part of installations, so don't try to rush.

Occasionally you will be able to remove the window frame (called the sash) from the building and take it back to your shop to install the window.

If the frame is wood and your window is only a single panel, requiring no T-bars to separate sections, then the process is to:
1. Remove the old putty or wooden "stops" that hold the old glass in place
2. Remove the old glass and all excess putty and glaziers points and clean and shellac the "rabbet" [rabbet: the groove cut into the sash for the glass to rest against - see photos]
3. Fit the leaded glass panel into the rabbet, trimming the outside lead where necessary
4. Tack the panel in place using #14 carpet tacks
5. Re-putty the sash using glazing compound and paint putty and sash if required.

Now, let's review those steps in detail, since they are, generally, the same proceses you'll use on all installations: preparing the sash, fitting the leaded glass and sealing against the weather.

Fig. 114 Using hacking knife.

Fig. 115 Using torch to soften putty.

Fig. 116 Using linoleum knife to remove softened putty.

Installation of Single Panel Window

1. Removing the old putty can be very time-consuming. Before the introduction of glazing compound, windows were puttied with linseed oil putty, made of linseed oil and whiting. This putty hardened in a few weeks and was difficult to remove. If it got too old and dry it would start to crack and lose its adhesion to the wood and fall off in chunks, allowing leaks to develop.

Today's glazing compounds take much longer to dry out and so are better sealants and much easier to remove. (Fig. 112) A hammer and putty chisel or hacking knife are the old stand-bys. (Fig. 113 and 114) A propane torch can help in heating up and softening the putty. (Fig. 115) Use a curved knife like a linoleum knife to cut the softened putty away. (Fig. 116) The heat of the torch will crack the old glass, so if you must save it, go back to the chisel. Electric putty heaters are available from glaziers supply dealers. (Fig. 117) Also available is a drill bit for use with an electric hand drill. It chips out putty, fast, in much the way a router cuts a groove in wood. (Fig. 118) All these methods work in some situations, but you'll find that you still use your chisel quite often.

2. Glaziers points hold the glass tight in the rabbet while the putty is being applied. They are small, flat ▲ or diamond ◆ shaped pieces of zinc and you should remove them next. If the glass is now loose, it can be removed in one piece, but often it will be stuck tight in putty and will, most likely, have to be broken out. Once the glass is removed, clean the entire rabbet of glass, glaziers points and putty. It is a good idea to seal the wood with shellac at this point. It protects the wood and keeps the oil in the fresh glazing compound from being absorbed into the wood.

112

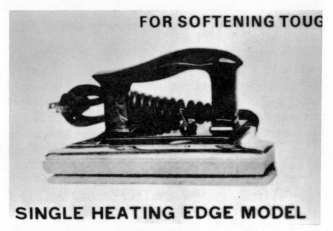

Fig. 117 Electric putty softener.

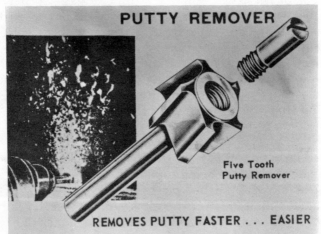

Adjustable guide screw prevents cutting into wood. Easily operated from either inside or outside of window. Used in conjunction with an electric drill, the "Somaca" Putty Remover will remove as much Putty in two minutes as one could remove in thirty minutes by the old method of wood chisel and hammer.

Fig. 118 Putty chipper.

3. Fit your panel into the rabbet. If it is too big in places or if the sash is not square you may have to trim your outside lead. Use a curved blade knife like a linoleum knife or a pruning knife. (Fig. 119) Rest the panel on edge and trim it, drawing the knife toward you. If this feels awkward to you, here's an alternative method: Lay the panel flat and use a utility knife to trim the lead one leaf at a time. Draw the knife along the lead where you want to cut it. This will make a mark on the lead. Follow that mark, making two or three strokes over and over, pressing gently. The top leaf will cut through and then you can do the same to the bottom leaf. (Fig. 120) Laying the panel flat to trim it is safer and you can be more accurate in your trimming. When the panel fits in the rabbet, mark the inside of the sash where your reinforcing bars will go. If you are using flat stiffening bars, then simply notch the sash so that they fit. If you are using saddle bars, then drill holes in the sash to accept the saddle bars. Make the hole deeper on one side so that you can push the bar into the deep hole and slide it back into the shallow hole on the opposite side.

Now fit your panel and check that your reinforcing bars line up either with the notches if you have flat stiffening bars, or with the banding wires if you are using saddle bars.

4. Now use #14 carpet tacks to tack your panel firmly into the sash. Use one tack at each joint on the border lead. (Fig. 121) The tack can pierce the empty leaf of the lead, but be careful that the head of the tack does not catch the edge of a piece of glass since this could cause a crack. Use a large nail set to pound the tacks snugly in place. (Fig. 122)

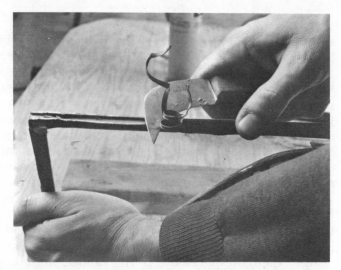

Fig. 119 Using linoleum knife to trim lead.

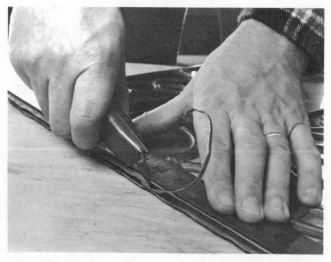

Fig. 120 Using utility knife and ruler to trim lead.

115

Fig. 121 Carpet tack holding the panel in the wood frame.

Fig. 122 Using a nail set to pound tacks.

Fig. 123 Glazing compound and bent putty knife.

5. Now you are ready to re-putty the sash to seal out the weather. Using glazing compound (Fig. 123) can be fun and is a real skill. Watch a real "putty-glazier" sometime for a treat.

If it is cold out you should open your glazing compound can and put it in a warm place as soon as you arrive at the site. When you are ready to use it, scoop out a wad the size of a tennis ball and roll it around in your hands till it is good and soft.

Use your thumb to apply blobs of glazing compound to the sash. (Fig. 124) This feels awkward at first, but if you practice you can get very fast.

117

Fig. 124 Applying glazing compound.

Fig. 125 *Running* a bead of glazing compound.

Fig. 126 *Finishing* a bead of glazing compound.

118

To smooth a bead of putty: use a stiff bent putty knife one inch wide. Start at the end furthest from you and draw the knife towards you while pressing it firmly against both the lead and the edge of the sash. This will leave a smooth bead of glazing compound (Fig. 125) filling the rabbet between the leaded glass and the sash. Now run your thumb lightly over this bead in the opposite direction (away from you). This will smooth it out even more. (Fig. 126)

Glazing compound can be painted immediately, and it is a good idea to do so. The paint seals the glazing compound, making it last longer.

Now if you are using saddle bars, it is time to wrap the banding wires around the bars and twist the ends together with pliers as shown. (Fig. 127) Do not twist them too tightly as you'll fatigue the copper and it will snap. Cut off the excess wire and fold the twisted wire back against the bar. (Fig. 128)

Fig. 127 Twisting banding wires.

Fig. 128 Fold wire to bar. **Fig. 129** Applying glazing compound to stops.

For wooden stops, apply glazing compound to the stop and press it tightly to the window and cut away excess glazing compound. (Fig. 129) If you are using wooden stops to hold your window in, then you might prefer to use caulking compound which comes in tubes (at the lumber yard) and is applied with a gun-type applicator. (Fig. 130)

Caulking compound is softer and you can apply it directly to the rabbet (Fig. 131), then press your wood stops tight against your leaded glass and clean off the excess caulking compound that oozes out.

120

Fig. 130 Latex caulking compound in gun, and silicone caulking compound.

Fig. 131 Applying caulking compound.

Fig. 132 Cutting away excess silicone caulk.

Caulking compound comes in different types. The putty type and rubber type. If you use the putty type, get the absolute best grade, since the cheaper ones tend to dry out quickly. The rubber type comes in butyl, latex and silicone. The butyl is a very good sealant, but very sticky and it is hard to remove the excess. I don't bother with it, for that reason. The latex is a good sealant and can be cleaned up with water or let dry for a few days until it becomes rubber and can be cut away neatly. The silicone is very expensive and the best sealer for any surface. It smells bad, is hard to clean up, but hardens in a few hours to a rubber which can be cut away neatly, and easily. (Fig. 132)

Removing stops that were sealed with rubber caulks is a really difficult job. The silicone is the most difficult, but they all have to be cut away with a razor blade. You should experiment and decide which is best for you.

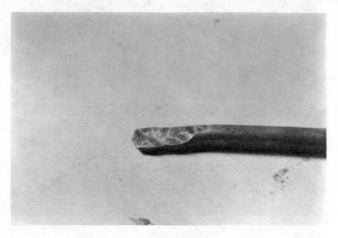

Fig. 133 Saddle bar pounded flat to fit under metal sash.

Fig. 134 Aluminum *sleeves* for saddle bar ends.

What you have learned so far will apply to all wood sash installations of single panels. In an aluminum or steel sash, the only real differences are that you can't notch the sash to fit the flat stiffening bar, or drill the sash for saddle bars or use carpet tacks to hold your window for puttying.

Flat stiffening bars must be cut off as shown, then soldered to panel so that the ends slip between the sash and the panel. (See Fig. 104)

Saddle bars can also be pounded flat on the ends (Fig. 133), or little sleeves can be made from aluminum tubing to fit around the bar and between the window and the sash. Get an aluminum tube that just fits around your saddle bar. Cut off a one inch piece of tubing and cut away the half cylinder section as shown using a hacksaw. Flatten the cut end and slip the whole end onto the saddle bar. (Fig. 134) The flattened tail will fit between the leaded glass and the metal sash. (Fig. 135)

Fig. 135 Sleeves slipped under metal frame.

Fig. 136 Metal sash clips and notched wood tool.

Instead of carpet tacks to hold your window in the metal sash while puttying, you must use "metal sash clips" which are bent pieces of copper wire which act as springs against your window. (Fig. 136) Drill holes along the length of the sash and apply the sash clips using a notched putty knife or piece of wood. (Figs. 137 and 138)

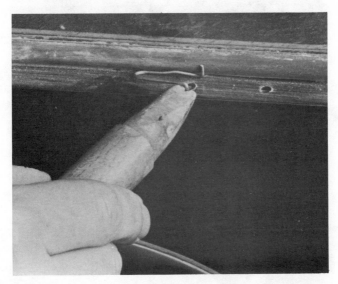

Fig. 137 Using tool to apply sash clip.

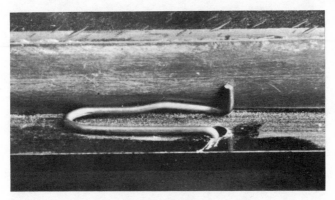

Fig. 138 Metal sash clip in place.

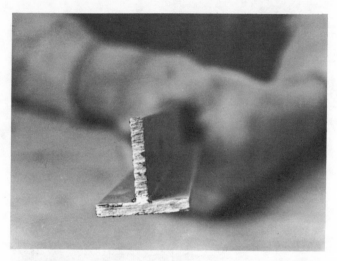

Fig. 139 1″ x 1″ x ⅛″ T-bar.

Fig. 140 T-bar screwed into notched wood frame.

Installing Multi-Panelled Windows

If the window opening is more than 48″ in *one* dimension, you should make your window in two or more panels.

If your window is smaller than 48″ in width or height, you will need T-bars in one direction only and you can install them in the frame yourself.

For instance, if your window is 24″ x 72″ you might want to make it in three panels, each 24″ x 24″ or perhaps two panels, each 24″ x 36″.

If your window is as wide as it is tall, say 48″ x 48″, you may decide that you would rather have the panels separated vertically; that is, three panels 48″ high and 16″ wide. (Each panel will still require reinforcing bars.) The panels will then be separated by 1″ x 1″ x ⅛″ steel or aluminum T-bar. (Fig. 139) I use aluminum because it's easier to cut and drill and won't rust. The T-bar will be installed in the frame so it forms a mullion against which the panel will rest. These mullions function the same as the mullions which separate the pieces of glass in a common household window sash.

Windows larger than 48″ in both *dimensions will need to have an armature of T-bar made to frame the four or more panels of the window. The T-bars will need to be welded where they cross. Call a welder.*

Fig. 141 T-bar installed in wood sash, ready to accept panels of stained glass. Notice the holes in the T-bar which will accept the sash clips.

Installing T-bar in Wood Sash or Frame

Cut T-bar to length to fit into rabbet in sash (same size as full-size of panel). Drill and countersink two holes at the end of T-bar. These holes are for screwing the T-bar to the wood sash. (Fig. 140)

Also drill several ⅛" holes (one every 8") in the tail of the T-bar about ½" from the face. These holes will accept the sash clips which will hold the panel in position while being puttied. Paint T-bars now.

Measure and mark the position of the T-bars on the frame and chisel a notch for the face of the T-bar to sit in ⅛" deep. (Fig. 140) Screw the T-bar in place, making sure it is level or plumb. The T-bar now forms a mullion for the panels to rest against. (Fig. 141)

Installing T-bar in Metal Sash

Cut the T-bar to full-size length, so that it fits into the rabbet. Drill the holes for the sash clips and paint T-bar. Now place the T-bar in position and mark the face where it meets the daylite size of the frame. Use a hack saw to remove the section of face from this mark to the end of the T-bar. Do the same to both ends. (Fig. 142)

Buy or make small angle brackets and attach one to each end of the T-bar using a small bolt and nut. (Fig. 143) The bracket can then be screwed into the metal frame using a sheet metal screw.

The lead at this corner of the panel will need to be trimmed a bit to fit over the bracket. *Once the T-bars are all in place you can proceed with installing the separate panels.* (Fig. 144)

Fig. 142 T-bar prepared for installation in metal frame.

Fig. 143 Small angle bracket attached to T-bar. *Courtesy K.C. Lewis.*

Fig. 144 Installing the individual panels.

AN ANNOTATED BIBLIOGRAPHY

of stained glass and related books.

Compiled with notes by Peter Mollica, © 1977

Introduction

Many of the books listed here are out of print and may be difficult to locate. Large booksellers will often have one or two and some booksellers will conduct a search for a particular book. I will try to indicate which are worth the search and the often high asking price.

The comments which follow titles are my own reactions to the book. This bibliography will be almost entirely of books in English. There exists a large selection of French and German books on stained glass. I've listed the ones I know if, but there are many others which bilingual readers will want to check out.

The existing literature on stained glass is very limited, consisting of many history and how-to-do-it books and very few criticism or design discussion books. There also exist many volumes which simply list by location the windows of an area and talk a bit about the theological subject matter of each. Many of these windows may no longer exist, so check the date of publication before setting out to see windows described. Lack of maintenance and lots of wars have caused the disappearance of many European windows.

I have been pretty lucky in finding many of the older books; there are, undoubtedly, lots that I've never heard of. You should not consider this bibliography complete, I don't. If there is an old stained glass studio near your home you should check with them. I've found that they are usually proud of their libraries and may turn you on to some good titles to search for. Try to be understanding if the owners of books you want to read are hesitant to lend them. As I've mentioned many are expensive and/or irreplaceable. So if you want to borrow, best do it from a library. If your dog chews up a copy of "Winston," you are not gong to be able to replace it.

If you come across a book which I have overlooked, and you think it valuable, please let me know about it.

The illustrations follow the book from which they were taken.

I have broken this bibliography into six sections:

1. Stained Glass: History 136
Books primarily devoted to history, although most contain sections on technique.

2. Stained Glass: How-To 155
Contain detailed descriptions of techniques. In dealing with the many how-to books on stained glass craft technique I have made clear which ones are most valuable and why. Some are just so-so and I have not given much space to these. Many are just a re-hash and don't offer a unique method of presentation or particularly good photographs. More often than not these probably represent yet another publisher seeking to cash in on a booming market.

Picture books of Twentieth Century work, discussion of design, books on particular stained glass artists.

A few titles on glass as a material.

The many books on Gothic churches, perhaps including some reference to the stained glass.

Modern architecture, and church building, theory and design. I feel that artists working in stained glass need to read extensively in the field of architecture. An awareness of architectural styles and practice will better enable one to design windows that relate directly to the intent of their settings. A window designed without thought to its eventual architectural setting will more than likely compete with the aesthetics of the architecture in ways that may be destructive both to environment and window. The design of church architecture has had the most direct influence on the design of stained glass. At the time of the gothic revival in this country, stained glass fit exactly the feeling of the mock-medieval architecture. Since that time, church architecture has been in a rather confused and undirected state. Except for certain isolated buildings, American churches have reflected a supreme lack of enthusiasm on the part of architects—and so with stained glass designers. In Europe, however, the church has remained an important part of the lives of the people and some strong styles of modern church design have resulted. Several of Europe's most exciting architects have contributed and, although much mediocre work [and a few disasters,] has been done, church architecture has remained alive and changing—and so with European stained glass design.

1. Stained Glass: History

- Alcaide V.N., RENAISSANCE STAINED GLASS IN SPAIN, Instituto Diego Velazquez, 1970, Madrid. Text in Spanish. Four color, 44 black and white photographs.
Renaissance Stained glass is not really a favorite of mine, but they sure could paint, especially faces. Effort was applied in great quantities to the painted details. Stained glass on the level of glass and lead design seemed to interest them much less.

- Amaya, M., THE TASTE OF TIFFANY, Apollo, February, 1965, pp. 102-109.
Article discussing the rekindled interest in Tiffany's art nouveau glass. Photograph of window made by Tiffany and designed by Pierre Bonnard.

- Amaya, Mario, TIFFANY GLASS, Walker and Company, New York, 1967.
Lots of photographs of vases and a few of windows and lamps and many pages of Tiffany talk.

- Ashdown, C.H., HISTORY OF THE WORSHIPFUL COMPANY OF GLAZIERS OF THE CITY OF LONDON, OTHERWISE THE COMPANY OF GLAZIERS AND PAINTERS OF GLASS, Blades, East and Blades, London, 1918.
Includes the "Minutes Book" from 1697, and a centerfold poster of "Prices of Glazier's Work," 1818. Interesting.

- Aubert, M., FRENCH CATHEDRAL WINDOWS OF THE 12th AND 13th CENTURIES, Iris Books, Oxford University Press, 1947, 19 color plates.
Very good color plates of all the biggies from 12th and 13th centuries—Bourges, Chartres, LeMans, etc.

- van Beuningen, C., STAINED GLASS WINDOWS, Academy Editions, London, 1972, 16 color plates.
Very good color of 12th to 15th century panels mostly from museums in Germany.

- Beyer, V., STAINED GLASS WINDOWS, Oliver and Boyd, London, 1964.

  Twenty-eight pages of history and technique and 60 good color plates including a 1954 window of Anton Wendling, an important figure in post-war German stained glass design.

- Bing, Samuel, ARTISTIC AMERICA, TIFFANY GLASS AND ART NOUVEAU, MIT Press, 1970.

  Articles written in 1895-1903 by Sam Bing, an art dealer from Paris. He was Tiffany's European distributor. In 1895, Bing returned from a trip to America and wrote the article "Artistic America" for the French Government. He picks American art that he likes in the fields of painting, sculpture, architecture and the industrial arts. In architecture his favorite was H. H. Richardson, but his overall favorite was L. C. Tiffany. He devoted a separate article to him in 1898. And it has some interesting old photographs of the glassblowing facilities at Tiffany Furnaces, Corona, New York. Essential reading for Tiffany freaks.

- Biedrzynski, R., FARBFENSTER GROKER KATHEDRALEN, Buchheim Verlag, 1965, text in German.

  One of the many "little books" of color photographs of ancient windows. Mostly details.

- Borias, G.A. and Cordeau, J., LE VITRAIL, Publications Filmees D'Art et D'Histoire, contains 24 color slides (35 mm).

  A little book made by the French Government and sold at the Musee de Cluny, Paris and other hot spots for stained glass tourists. French text discusses how glass is made at St. Gobain Glass Factory, how windows are made, history by century and commentaries on each of the 24 slides. Nice little book—they would sell lots if they published it in German and English as well.

- Braun, H.S., EIN KLEINES FARBENWUNDER, Aldus Manutius Verlag, Zurich, text in German.

  Thirty color photographs of the Gothic windows of "Der Kirche auf Dem Staufberg." Very simple, brightly colored figure windows with large-eyed white faces.

- CORPUS VITREARUM MEDII AEVI, Paris, various authors, various publishers.

  Twenty to thirty year survey of 12th to 16th Century stained glass in Europe country by country. Will comprise 75 volumes when complete. So unbelievably expensive that you'll have to rely on libraries for these, and probably only the biggest libraries will get it all. Try universities and religious schools.

- Day, Lewis F., STAINED GLASS, Chapman and Hall, Ltd., London, 1903.

  History by periods, a handbook for the collection of the Victoria and Albert Museum. Most of the illustrations are from glass in the museum.

- Day, Lewis F., WINDOWS: A BOOK ABOUT STAINED AND PAINTED GLASS, B. T. Batsford, London, 1909.

  Lots of black and white illustrations. Lots of interesting comment on history and specific windows. At the end of his 403 pages Day closes with this thought, "we ride our hobbies to death, of course; but it is only human to hope that what interested and absorbed me so cannot be without interest to some others."

- Delaporte, Y., L'ART DU VITRAIL AUX 12e et 13e SIECLES, Editions Houvet, Chartres, 1963.
  Booklet available at the Cathedral. Sixteen color photographs and many black and whites of Chartres. French text in two sections: 1. Materials and techniques and 2. Sources of inspiration.

- Dierick, Alfons, THE STAINED GLASS AT CHARTRES, Hallwag, Berne.
  A little book with 19 color close-ups of the ancient glass accompanied by a short description. An introduction gives the history of the windows and explains how they were made in the 12th century.

- Drake, Maurice, A HISTORY OF ENGLISH GLASS-PAINTING, T. Werner Laurie, Ltd., London, 1912.
  A history designed to inform collectors of old stained glass. Where to find it and what to look for.

- Dürst, H., ANCIENT STAINED GLASS OF SWITZERLAND, Office du Livre, 1971, text in French and German. Twenty color and 40 black and white photographs.
  Again the 14th century windows from the cloister at Konigsfelden stand with the best from France and England. Look for this in English translation; I think it's available.

- Eden, F.S., ANCIENT STAINED AND PAINTED GLASS, University Press, Cambridge, 1913 and 1933.
  Discusses the "fragmentary condition and the historical causes which have produced that condition" (of Ancient stained glass), then gives history of different styles, and suggestions regarding preservation of ancient glass.
  The 1933 edition contains 6 color plates and an appendixed article on "Foreign Influences on Native English Glass-painting in the Late 15th and 16th Centuries."

• Farmer, O.G., FAIRFORD CHURCH AND ITS STAINED GLASS WINDOWS, to be obtained at the Home Cafe (opposite the church), High Street, Fairford, Glouchestershire.

History and description of the ancient glass which includes lots of really imaginative painted devils. These are some very finely painted windows, but they are not in great shape. The Last Judgment west window has been very well published in photographs, especially the red devils in the lower right section. In real life it is somewhat deteriorated—but still very powerful—one of the masterpieces of stained glass.

• Franks, A.W., ORNAMENTAL GLAZING QUARRIES, COLLECTED AND ARRANGED FROM ANCIENT EXAMPLES, J. H. Parrer, London, 1849.

One hundred and twelve full size drawings of medieval quarries each with a painted decoration. Name of church where original can be found is given.

A great book!

- Gaudin, Felix, LE VITRAIL DU 12ᵉ AU 18ᵉ SIECLES EN FRANCE, Flammarion, Paris, 1928. Text in French.
Fifty-seven black and white photographs and a history by century.

- Harries, John, DISCOVERING STAINED GLASS, Shire Publishes, Tring Herts, England, 1968. Sixteen black and white photographs.
Written as a tour guide to stained glass in English churches with a list by county of interesting stained glass. The text starts out with a discussion of damage and restoration over the centuries, then takes us back to medieval times. An interesting account of the inflations of the square foot price for stained glass from 13d in the 14th century to 1s in the 15th and sky-rocketing to 1s.6d. in the 16th century. Also sections on how windows were made and a brief history.
The publisher also has a little book titled, DISCOVERING BELLS AND BELLRINGING, which is fascinating.

- Houvet, Etienne, CHARTRES SES VITRAUX, Editions Houvet, Chartres.
One of the many booklets available at the Cathedral. This one has many color photographs of close-ups of the stained glass. Short French text.

- Hutchinson, MEDIEVAL GLASS AT ALL SOULS COLLEGE, Faber and Faber, London, circa 1950.
Descriptions of the windows. Black and white photographs.

- Hutter, Heribert, MEDIEVAL STAINED GLASS, Crown Publishers, Inc., New York, 1963.
Twenty-four color photographs of ancient stained glass. Mostly details. Also a short history.

- Johnson, J.R., THE RADIANCE OF CHARTRES, Random House, New York City, 1965.
Thorough study of stained glass of Chartres. Trying to explain why it is better than any other.
Discusses the experience of seeing the windows, the theories of Viollet-le-Duc, the glass itself as a material with some great micro photographs of the glass, and finally the color choice and composition of the windows.
A must!

- Kieslinger, Franz, GLASMALEREI IN ÖSTERREICH (Glass-painting in Austria), Kunstverlag Wolfrum, Wien, 1947.

  Forty-eight photographs, 12 in color, of old Austrian windows. Pretty good pictures of these Austrian windows which you won't see published many other places.

- Knowles, J.A., THE YORK SCHOOL OF GLASS PAINTING, Society for Promoting Christian Knowledge, London, 1936 (Also MacMillan Co., New York).

  Lots of local York history and details like costs in Shillings and Pence of windows.

  Good drawings from medieval windows.

- Koch, R., LOUIS TIFFANY, REBEL IN GLASS, Crown Publishers, New York City, 1964.

  Biography and discussion of his work.

  A few good color photographs and many black and white photographs of Tiffany studios work and photographs of historic interest. My favorite is a photograph of 10 workmen each working on a Tiffany lamp.

- Koch, R., LOUIS C. TIFFANY'S GLASS-BRONZES-LAMPS, A COMPLETE COLLECTORS GUIDE, Crown Publishers, New York City, 1971.

  Photographs and descriptions of hundreds of objects turned out by Tiffany studios. Includes a price list of 1906.

- Lasteryie, HISTOIRE DE LA PEINTURE SUR VERRE, 2 volumes, Firmin-Didot Fréres, Paris, 1853.
The classic French history of medieval stained glass. I don't read French easily so I have never read this, but it would be interesting to compare the French view with the more familiar English view.

- Le Couteur, J.D., ENGLISH MEDIEVAL PAINTED GLASS, Society for Promoting Christian Knowledge, 1926.
A little technique and lots of history.

- Lee, Lawrence, THE APPRECIATION OF STAINED GLASS, Oxford University Press, London, 1977.
I just got this book from the publisher today, so I haven't read it. In the introduction, Lee says: "The intention of this book is to assist an active appreciation of English stained glass." Most of the illustrations are of ancient glass, or ancient-style glass.

- Lee, L.; Seddon, G.; Stephans, F.; STAINED GLASS, Crown Publishers, Inc., New York, 1976, Mitchell-Beazley Publishers, London, 1976. Photos by Sonia Halliday and Laura Lushington.
This is the prettiest history of stained glass you are likely to find. It includes hundreds of superb photographs and a very slick presentation. My own prejudices make me think that the sections on 20th century Germany and U.S.A. are very sparse, but this probably reflects the fact that the English stained glass world has only recently become aware of what's been going on next door.

The format is very attractive. Every two pages are treated as an essay on some subject: "Glass in the Ancient World;" "The Language of Symbols;" "Faces of Christ;" "The Ancient Traditions of Heraldry;" "The World's Oldest Windows;" "The Age of Gothic Art;" "The Glory of French Glass;" "Master Glaziers in Merchant Cities;" "Tiffany— Creator of Opulence;" "Adapting an Ancient Art;" are a few. This format is a relief from the usual dull presentation of history. Excellent distribution and an up-to-date presentation will make this the most read version of the history of stained glass. It will undoubtedly be referred to as the definitive statement for some time to come.

A contribution to the history of humor (unintentional) in stained glass can be seen on p. 57 . . . The window from Canterbury depicting George VI and Princess Elizabeth.

Like virtually all stained glass books (except Rigan's NEW GLASS) this one couldn't resist a how-to-do-it chapter. They also have a very interesting section on restoration of ancient windows, a cursory gazetteer of stained glass by country and a glossary.

- Lewis, Mostyn, STAINED GLASS IN NORTH WALES UP TO 1850, John Sherratt and Son, Ltd., 1970.
  Seventy-two black and white photographs of details.
  Brief history of the Wales glass, then descriptions of glass by church and town.

- Marchini, G., ITALIAN STAINED GLASS WINDOWS, H. Abrams, New York City, 1956, ninety-three color plates, four color transparencies.
  Good color photographs of all the best of the ancient stained glass of Italy 13th to 16th centuries. These windows have a different feeling from the French and German—not so Gothic, as we are used to thinking of it.

- Musée des Arts Décoratifs de Paris, LE VITRAIL FRANÇAIS, Éditions des Deux Mondes, 1968.
  Primarily a history and analysis of the ancient stained glass of France, with a final chapter on modern trends which includes discussion of Manessier and Matisse. The real value of the book is the illustrations—32 color, 236 black and white.

- Nelson, P., ANCIENT PAINTED GLASS IN ENGLAND, 1170-1500, Methuen and Company, Ltd., London, 1913.

  History and county lists of stained glass with a brief chapter on restoration

- Oidtmann, H., STAINED GLASS OF THE 12th-16th CENTURIES IN THE RHINELAND, Düsseldorf, 1929, German text.

  History—I wish it were in English.

- Rackham, B., THE ANCIENT GLASS OF CANTERBURY CATHEDRAL, Lund Humphries and Company, Ltd., London, 1949.

  A thorough history and description of Canterbury's glass, which is now being restored at great cost. If you can't find a copy of this book, you might send the money to the restoration fund for the cathedral windows.

- Rackham, B., GUIDE TO THE COLLECTIONS OF STAINED GLASS, VICTORIA AND ALBERT MUSEUM, London, 1936.

  Published by the Museum to catalog its excellent collection of ancient stained glass.

- Read, H., J. Baker, A. Lammer, ENGLISH STAINED GLASS, Thames and Hudson, London, 1960 (Also H. Abrams, New York City), 34 color, 103 black and white.

  The best of the picture books of ancient stained glass. The black and white detail photographs are among the best photographs of stained glass I've seen.

  The color frontispiece and p. 153 show details of the west window at St. Mary's church, Fairford, Gloucestershire, in my opinion the highlights of this book and well worth the cost of searching for a copy.

  The text is a pretty authoritative history of English stained glass. A must!

- Read, H. ENGLISH STAINED GLASS, G. P. Putnam's Sons, London and New York, 1926.

  Reprinted: circa 1975. I haven't seen this book and the reprint is circa $50, so I'm waiting for my library to get it.

- Saint, L. and Arnold, H., STAINED GLASS OF THE MIDDLE AGES IN ENGLAND AND FRANCE, Adam and Charles Black, London, 1913.
  A little technique and lots of history.

- Schmutzler, Robert, ART NOUVEAU, Harry N. Abrams, Inc., New York, 1964.
  My reason for including this book is the same as my reason for buying it—the good color photograph on p. 243 of Charles Rennie Macintosh's doors for the Willow Tea Rooms in Glasgow. There are some other photographs of stained glass in the book as well as good photographs of most of the great works in art nouveau style.

- Schultz, Simone, GLASFENSTER DES STRASS-BURGER MÜNSTERS, Verlag Hallweg, Stuttgart, 1967.
  A little book with 19 color close-ups of windows from Strassburg Cathedral.

- Sewter, A. Charles, THE STAINED GLASS OF WILLIAM MORRIS AND HIS CIRCLE, Yale University Press, New Haven, 1974. A second volume will be published as a catalogue of Morris windows.
  If William Morris is your cup of tea, then this is *the* book for you. For me Morris and Company's windows have always meant: The exquisite draughtsmanship and sweet faces of Burne-Jones placed on the leafy decorative backgrounds of William Morris, expertly crafted. That's actually only a small part of what they did, and this book set me straight. The rougher, more emotional work of Madox Brown is very strong, though it appears that Burne-Jones was much the favored designer. Another thing I'd always associated with Morris windows was the clumsy chopping up of the figures with leadlines unrelated to anatomical or drapery design. This was, undoubtedly, so that none of the delicate rendering of the folds would be obscured by the heavy lead line. An attitude evident in the many cartoons reproduced here showing no leadlines at all. It was presumably the job of some lesser mortal to fill in the leadlines later in a craftsmanlike manner. However they did it, they always succeeded in filling their windows with the spirit of the Victorian Era—so much so that they now stand as a major symbol of that time in England.

- Sherrill, C.H., STAINED GLASS TOURS OF SPAIN AND FLANDERS, John Lane, The Bodley Head, London, 1924.

  Also; by the same author:
  STAINED GLASS TOURS OF ENGLAND, 1910
  STAINED GLASS TOURS OF FRANCE, 1922
  STAINED GLASS TOURS OF ITALY, GERMANY, AUSTRIA, AND RHINELANDS, 1927.

  City to city, church to church, romantic tours between the wars. I've never used these books as tour guides, and in fact I find them difficult to read, so much description of subject matter.

- Stettler, M., SWISS STAINED GLASS OF THE 14th CENTURY FROM THE CHURCH OF KÖNIGS-FELDEN, B. T. Batsford Ltd., London, 1949, 16 large color plates.

  Very good color plates of 14th century windows at Koenigsfelden which are beautiful and in very good condition.

- Theophilus, ON DIVERS ARTS, University of Chicago Press, 1963. Translation by J. Hawthorne and C. Smith.

  The true date and author are not known. The earliest manuscripts are 12th century, no original has survived. Consists of three books, the arts of painting, glass, and metal. The original stained glass how-to-do-it book.

  Tells the craftsman how to: Build a furnace, make the glass in colored sheets, make jugs, make mosaic tile, all the processes of making a stained glass window including casting lead came, repair a broken glass jug, make a glass finger ring.

- Tiffany Studios, A PARTIAL LIST OF WINDOWS, Published originally in 1910 by Tiffany studios and reprinted in 1973 from the original in the Boston Public Library by Tiffany Press, Watertown, Massachusetts.

  Originally published as an advertising catalog, it now serves as a tour guide for Tiffany lovers. A bit frustrating, though, as many of the churches have long since disappeared and taken their windows with them.

- Viollet-Le-Duc, E.E., 1875, VITRAIL (Translation by Francis Smith, 1942, of article on medieval stained glass in the "Dictionnaire Raisonné de L'Architecture Française du XIe Au XVIe Siecle."

Viollet-Le-Duc's studies of medieval architecture are classics—this very close study of medieval stained glass is referred to by most authors writing after him on the subject.

For discussion of his theories, see:
  Johnson, J.R., THE RADIANCE OF CHARTRES
  Sowers, R., THE LOST ART
  Sowers, R., STAINED GLASS AN ARCHITECTURAL ART
  THE ART BULLETIN, THE STAINED GLASS THEORIES OF VIOLLET-LE-DUC, Vol XLV, #2, June, 1963, p. 123.

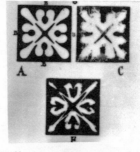

- Warrington, William, THE HISTORY OF STAINED GLASS, FROM THE EARLIEST PERIOD OF THE ART TO THE PRESENT TIME, Published by the author, Berkeley Street West, London, 1848, 16" x 24", illustrated with Chroma-lithography plates of the author's windows.

Warrington starts by dedicating his book to the Queen (Victoria, that is). He then explains how it all came about and why it is illustrated only with his own windows though it is a history of the entire art. I won't tell you how he gets himself out of that one. He then elegantly apologizes for his lack of literary elegance, explains that "The true and only standard of excellence is the medieval style of art," decries the work of many "modern artists" and proceeds with his history of stained glass. This is quite a feat of book production containing huge color reproductions and bound with leather and gold edged paper. I was equally impressed by the author's windows in Ely Cathedral done in 13th century style, prior to the re-discovery of medieval glass making techniques.

Because of the high quality of production and the size of this book and its fold-out color printing from 1848, and the small number of copies printed, it falls into the category of "rare books." This means that it will be next to impossible to find and will cost about $200—or more if you find one. If your interest is stained glass and not old books than I'd recommend that you don't even bother looking for this one. It is interesting mostly as a curiosity; the information it contains is available in many easier-to-find books.

- Werck, A., STAINED GLASS: A HANDBOOK ON THE ART OF STAINED GLASS AND PAINTED GLASS, ITS ORIGIN AND DEVELOPMENT FROM THE TIME OF CHARLEMAGNE TO ITS DECA-DENCE, (850-1650 A.D.), Nicholas Brown, New York City, 1922.
  History by an American glass worker. List of glass artists 14th to 17th centuries. Also after page 132 there is a photograph of the smallest glass panel in existence, a crucifixion scene by the author.

- Westlake, N.H.J., A HISTORY OF PAINTED GLASS, 4 vols., James Parker and Company, London, 1881.
  These volumes are, as the title conveys, a history of stained glass, and long considered the authoritative one, at least from the English point of view.

- Winston, Chas., AN INQUIRY INTO THE DIFFERENCE OF STYLE OBSERVABLE IN ANCIENT GLASS PAINTINGS ESPECIALLY IN ENGLAND: WITH HINTS ON GLASS PAINTING BY AN AMATEUR, J. H. Parker, Oxford, 1846, Part I - Text, Part II - Plates.

Winston went around looking at glass and drawing what he saw, he gained much knowledge and was instrumental in the beginnings of the blown sheet glass revival in England in mid 19th century.

It is obvious that he looked very closely at medieval glass and his drawings are exquisite. Part I includes a translation of Theophilus' treatise on working with glass.

A must!

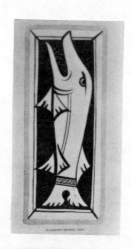

- Winston, Chas., MEMOIRS ILLUSTRATIVE OF THE ART OF GLASS PAINTING, John Murray, Albemarle Street, London, 1865. Published by his friends after his death.

Includes a short biography of Winston and a series of letters written about Glasgow Cathedral, descriptions with drawings of windows in England and a lecture delivered in 1859 on glass painting.

A classic! One of the essential documents of modern stained glass.

- Winter, Henry, THE DYNASTY OF LOUIS COMFORT TIFFANY FINAL EDITION, Henry Winter, Boston, 1971.

This book is the effort of a man devoted to the memory of L. C. Tiffany. His brother, William Winter, was the supervisor of Tiffany's interior decoration department at his Madison Avenue studios. This is really a scrapbook of fond memories and personal events. The photographs are not always of the best quality as some are reproductions of old Tiffany catalogs. But there's lots of them and I'm sure this book is a gold mine for Tiffany freaks.

- Witzleben, E., STAINED GLASS IN FRENCH CATHEDRALS, Thames and Hudson, London, 1968.

Forty-six color transparencies and 96 black and white photographs of ancient windows.

A flashy new book which already went out of print and I think is about to be reissued.

- Woodforde, C., ENGLISH STAINED GLASS AND GLASS PAINTERS OF THE 14th CENTURY, British Academy, 1939.

Lecture with 8 black and white photographs.

Dr. Woodforde offers the interesting theory that even in the 14th century the development of style in stained glass lagged somewhat behind that of the other arts. Interesting history, specifically England, but it's easy to imagine yourself sitting in an uncomfortable chair in a lecture hall thoroughly bored with the subject and wishing there were more than eight photographs to illustrate the 7000 words. There is a good chance that in January, 1939, one's mind might have been on other things. I could be wrong because Dr. Woodforde obviously loves his subject and may have been an engaging speaker.

- Woodforde, C., ENGLISH STAINED AND PAINTED GLASS, Oxford University Press, 1954.

History Century by Century, 12th to 20th. 80 black and white photographs. County list of places containing stained glass illustrated in this book.

A quote I liked from his preface, "A window may be odious; but it must be intrinsically odious, not odious by comparison."

152

- Young, Mary, SINGING WINDOWS, Abingdon Press, New York City, 1962.
Stained glass history and romance for kids.

Magazines

- ART AND ARCHAEOLOGY, June, 1927, pp. 243-259, "Notes on the Historic Stained Glass of Northern France."
Some photographs show destruction of stained glass at Rheims and other French churches during World War I.

- BULLETIN, Metropolitan Museum of Art, December, 1971/January, 1972.
Catalog for exhibition of ancient stained glass at the cloisters in New York City, 1972. Some excellent photographs and a good introduction to the history of stained glass.

- Burgess, I., "Stained Glass," MENTOR, December,
  1919.
  Brief history, a list of "characteristic and important windows" for different periods of glass design. Short articles on stained glass in France, England, Italy, the Netherlands, the Rhine countries and America.

- Burgess, I., "Heraldic Design in Stained Glass," INTERIOR STUDIO, February, 1928.
  Heraldic descriptions and black and white photographs of 6 windows including one of the oldest examples of heraldry in stained glass which is now at the Metropolitan Museum of Art, New York City.

- Connick, Charles J., " 'La Belle Verriere' of Infinite Quality," THE AMERICAN MAGAZINE OF ART, Metropolitan Museum, New York, March, 1932.
  An article and paintings of "La Belle Verriere" of Chartres by Connick.

- Connick, Charles J., "Windows of Old France," INTERNATIONAL STUDIO, December 1923; January 1924; July 1924; New York.
  These articles are three of a series of four which Connick did for this magazine. I do not know the date of the fourth. These three discuss the ancient glass of Notre Dame de Paris, St. Chapelle, St. Denis, Chartres and have black and white and some color photographs.

- Eden, F.S., "Heraldic Stained Glass at Gray's Inn," CONNOISSEUR, July, 1936.
  Heraldic description and some black and white photographs of interest mostly to heraldry fanatics; the stained glass is not so great.

- Hutchinson, G.P., "Liverpool's Stained Glass," INTERNATIONAL STUDIO, October 1925, New York.
  The stained glass at the Anglican Cathedral of Liverpool is discussed and pictured. Of the James Powell and Sons/Whitefriars windows the author concludes: "The windows of Liverpool Cathedral may be said to mark a new epoch in glass, for they carry on the true Gothic spirit, but expressed in the language of today; modern in drawing and execution and free from any affectation of medievalism."

- LITHOPINION 24, "A Portfolio of Medieval Stained Glass," (Magazine of Amalgamated Lithographers of America), Winter, 1971, Vol. 6, #4, Issue 24, pp. 16-31.

  Excellent photographs of medieval windows taken from "English Stained Glass" by Baker and Lammer.

  Same issue also contains an article by R. Morris, "The Rebirth of a 'Dead' Art." (Meaning stained glass)

  Same issue also contains great photographs of the Wright Brothers' first flights—essential to stained glass enthusiasts.

- Mélikian, S., "Close-up of 10 Centuries of Stained Glass," RÉALITÉS, April, 1966.

  A short review of a Strasbourg show of stained glass with some very colorful details of windows.

- PARIS MATCH, "La Grande Rose de Notre Dame," 27 Dec. 1969, pp. 30-37.

  Good photographs of some of the windows of Notre Dame, Paris.

- Reynolds, J.G., Jr., "Stained Glass," Parts 1-5, THE AMERICAN ARCHITECT AND THE ARCHITECTURAL REVIEW, Vol. CXXL, Numbers 2394, 2395, 2396, 2398, 2399.

  Technique and history and decorative possibilities of stained glass in five parts by Joseph Reynolds, one of the early exponents of the neo-gothic style of stained glass in America. He worked in a 13th or 14th century style.

- Vilardebo, Jeanne, "When the Lights Went up all over Europe," RÉALITÉS, August, 1969.

  Excellent color photographs of ancient windows and an historical text telling about the new museum in Darmstadt, Germany, which houses all this old stained glass and one or two 20th century pieces.

2. Stained Glass: How-To

- Armitage, E. Liddall, STAINED GLASS, Charles T. Branford Company, Newton, Massachusetts, 1959.

  I've always liked this book because it was the first book I read about stained glass and it got me interested enough to do something about it. I read it over and over, especially the parts on technique. Of course, I was surprised a year or two later when I began my apprenticeship and found that reality was in many cases quite different from what this book had taught me. I was in America and the book had been written in England, so I found no gas soldering iron and got laughs when I asked about tracing linen. But for me this book had done its job and more—it had moved me to find out for myself, not a bad goal for any author.

  The final chapter gives a short section written by some of the author's favorite stained glass artists. They include names which I was to hear over and over again. In general, the book has a very traditional approach and in 1959, it summed up what had been said so often before on history, technique and how to design for an east light or a south light, etc., etc.

  Other stained glass people who have no emotional attachment to this book tell me they don't like it much.

- Berlye, Milton, ENCYCLOPEDIA OF WORKING WITH GLASS, Oceana Publishers, New York, 1968, Book 1 and 2 in one volume.

  Book 1: Cutting, drilling, forming, blowing, firing, shaping, decorating, engraving, frosting, chipping, edging, joining, mending, and other related information.

Book 2: Glass activities for schools, studios, camps, homes, and all types of activity centers—and information about glass.

Also an index and glossary.

pp. 188-198 deal specifically with stained glass windows and how they are made. The steps in window making are discussed and illustrated with photographs of workers in the Payne-Spiers stained glass studio.

pp. 199-204 deal with a particularly ugly form of simulated stained glass.

pp. 205-208 describes methods of making slab glass window panels using both 1" thick slab glass or normal ⅛" thick antique.

Other chapters of interest discuss mosaic, mirror making, enamelling, fiberglass, glass-blowing at Steuben Glass Works, glass blowing for laboratories, sagging in molds, cutting windshield glass.

- Clow, B. and G., STAINED GLASS: A BASIC MANUAL, Little, Brown and Company, Boston, 1976.

The author claims to be introducing in this book the technique of cutting glass without patterns using a light box beneath her cartoon with the glass laid on top and cut. This is essentially the same method used in English studios for years, perhaps centuries. She then asks you to have a "beginner's mind" as a Zen monk and "put yourself totally into Barbara's hands." I say, "Don't do it." The author seems inexperienced and the text is loaded with errors and misconceptions.

- Divine, J., and Blachford, G., STAINED GLASS CRAFT, F. Warne and Company, Ltd., London, 1940—Republished Dover, New York, 1972.

A small textbook covering all the steps of the craft from design to installation. Also has a chapter on other projects with glass and one on stained glass as a school craft.

Very traditional approach, I like the drawings.

- Duval, Jean-Jacques, WORKING WITH STAINED GLASS, Thomas Crowell Company, New York, 1972.
  This book introduces the novice to the essentials of making leaded glass window panels. It also describes techniques for laminating glass to glass, building a slab-glass panel, and construction of a lampshade using copper foil. The photographs and drawings are very good. The photographs are taken as you would view the action while doing it as though the camera were mounted on your forehead. There are also many photographs of unusual hobby work. A good first book.

- Erikson, Erik, STEP-BY-STEP STAINED GLASS, A COMPLETE INTRODUCTION TO THE CRAFT OF STAINED GLASS, Golden Press, New York, 1974.
  Some of the many color photographs are of interest. Erikson shows work of some good modern designers including his own. On p. 33 he has a photograph of a window by Sam Weiner which is a favorite of mine. His how-to section covers copper foil, slab glass, laminated glass, crushed glass, glass mosaic, glass sandwiching, as well as traditional leaded glass techniques.

- French, Jennie, GLASS-WORKS, THE COPPER FOIL TECHNIQUE OF STAINED GLASS, Van Nostrand Reinhold Company, New York, 1974.
  How-to with copper foil. Interesting comments and drawing of small studio set-up, a section on "shop-yoga," a start at designing, and a chapter called "first works" which shows a 9-year-old girl doing a great job on her first stained glass piece.

- Gick, James, CREATING WITH STAINED GLASS, Future Crafts Today, Laguna Beach, California, 1976.
  All the photographs, including the instruction sections, are in color. My favorite is the one on p. 23 showing the purple glass being stabbed by the glass cutter held in a green hand. Very interesting photographs of machine made glass and lead came being made at Hollander Glass Company.

- Hanks, K., Belliston, L., Edwards, D., DESIGN YOURSELF, William Kaufman, Inc., One First Street, Los Altos, California, 1977.

  This book does not deal with stained glass specifically. I don't know if you can learn to design stained glass from a book. The books I've seen which attempt to teach it seem limited and unsuccessful. There are techniques and attitudes which all designers use, these can be communicated.

  As an introduction to the processes of design, in general, I think this is a good book. The authors insist that "we are all designers" and they explain how sucessful designs come from around and inside ourselves . . . instead of out of a pattern book.

- Holiday, H., STAINED GLASS AS AN ART, MacMillan, London, 1896.

  Speaking of early 19th century stained glass, Holiday says, "In the whole black list of offenses for which trade is responsible there is probably nothing which for its enduring odiousness can compare with the sacrilegious desecration of our noblest buildings unblushingly carried on for money—profit through a considerable part of this century."

  This book discusses: Materials and techniques, artistic possibilities in stained glass in relation to technique, artistic possibilities in stained glass in relation to situation and purpose of the work. Photographs of Burne-Jones designs for stained glass.

- Isenberg, Anita and Seymour, HOW TO WORK IN STAINED GLASS, Chilton Book Company, New York, 1972.

  I have never liked this book, the level of imagination used in the designs presented is very low. Some of the misleading information, like describing the use of what they call "cleaning and polishing powder" and not telling the reader he can use whiting or plaster of paris makes me angry. Also misleading is their discussion of flux on pages 27, 28, 92, 93, and 97. All this amounts to telling one that only their specific flux is going to work. What is it? Just in case they go out of business? Well, the main ingredient is oleic acid, but to get it to flow smoothly and evenly it is "mixed with other material." What other material, you ask? Shut up and buy!

Their approach makes this book a sales pitch for the authors' mail-order supply shop. It treats stained glass as a "gift-shop craft." I guess if you already own the book then you can dig out the information you need, but I can see no reason for buying it. In fairness though, Chapter 3 contains a good bit of technical information about solder composition and melting temperatures.

- Judson, Walter, INTRODUCTION TO STAINED GLASS, A STEP-BY-STEP GUIDE, Nash Publishing, Los Angeles, 1972.

This is the only how-to book I've seen which shows you how to make your own glazing knife from a cut-off putty knife. This is lots of fun to do, but here you're working with molten lead so be sure you don't breathe the fumes.

- Kinney, Kay, GLASS CRAFT, Chilton Book Company, New York, 1962.

Best known for her fused glass techniques, but this book covers lots more, like cutting, drilling, molds for slumping, glazes and enamels.

- Lee, L., STAINED GLASS, Oxford University Press, London, 1967.

"This book is written for those who seriously want to become professional stained glass artists . . . ," Lee starts his book with this phrase. He suggests a trip to Chartres Cathedral and then one's local (English) parish church. He takes us on an imaginary tour of such a church, describing the social history which has brought the church and its windows to its present state. He follows this with a brief history in a similar tour guide fashion. Not as dry as most and far more readable, I think it is plenty for a start. I like my history in small entertaining doses. His final section on modern work talks about Coventry Cathedral, Leger in France, and John Piper in England.

Chapter Two is on technique: materials, tools, studio equipment, miscellaneous materials, are first described and then the processes of a leaded window, a slab glass window, a glass on glass applique window, sand-blasting and engraving and sculptures.

Chapter Three is on design. Lee starts by describing some of the analysis that had to be done in designing the windows for Coventry. The remainder of the design chapter is broken into sections dealing with 1. color, 2. juxtaposition, 3. halation, 4. glass painting. Number 4, glass painting, is obviously the most important of these to Mr. Lee. He discusses the traditional uses of paint. He closes by suggesting an exercise in collage to develop a design for a first panel.

Chapter Four on training and professional practice says go to an art school but don't forget tradition. He then talks about the mechanics of commissioning as practiced by churches and resumes the tour guide stance and leads us through a job from start to finish. A section on architects advises learning their language and problems. He concludes with a question and long answer section.

- Lips, Claude, ART AND STAINED GLASS, Doubleday and Company, New York, 1973.

  This book doesn't really mention "art" at all, what the title is trying to say is "art glass." It's a how-to book.

- Luciano, STAINED GLASS WINDOW ART, Hidden House/Flash Books, Palo Alto, California, 1974.

  A how-to section followed by patterns of old-fashioned windows and color pictures of the work of seven stained glass artists, I'm sorry to say that I'm one of them. The presentation and color printing is horrible.

- Metcalf, MAKING STAINED GLASS, McGraw-Hill, New York, 1972.

  Complete "handbook," MAKING STAINED GLASS by Robert and Gertrude Metcalf goes into detail on history, materials, tools, the professional studio, glass painting, etching, cementing and installing of stained glass windows.

  The Metcalfs preface most of their chapters with an excerpt from Theophilus, who wrote a how-to-make-stained glass book in the 11th century or thereabouts. Theophilus, being a bit of a dilettante, left out lots of important information which the Metcalfs fill in nicely, including some good photographs of sheet glass being blown at Blenko Glass Co. in West Virginia. In a chapter devoted to lead came, the Metcalfs describe lead milling equipment and recommend it highly for small studios, suggesting that we buy up plumbing from old houses to get lead. The expense of the equipment and the time involved in making one's own lead came has stopped most studios. Perhaps the price increases on extruded came will make it more feasible. I doubt it.

The strongest section of this book seems to me to be the glass painting section. They offer lots of new information which they have sought out for their own use, especially about the preparation of the tracing and matting paints. They are very specific about which tools and methods they have found most satisfactory. The traditional techniques which they teach lend themselves neatly to the more or less gothic styles of stained glass windows. For most of us there is enough to learn here to keep us busy for a lifetime. However, there is a lot to be done with paint that no one has done yet, and I'm not sure that if you wish to take that direction it might not be better to ignore these traditional techniques altogether. With new epoxy paints, etc., you might even be able to throw the old kiln into the studio dump. Don't be too rough with it though, your apprentice's apprentice will want to rediscover it in years to come.

(Taken from my review of this book in the February, 1974, GLASS ART MAGAZINE, with thanks.)

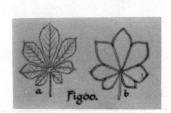

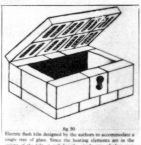

fig 50
Electric flash kiln designed by the authors to accommodate a single tray of glass. Since the heating elements are in the ceiling of the kiln, it will fire the single tray of glass very rapidly.

- Mollet, Ralph, LEADED GLASS WORK, Sir Isaac Pitman and Sons, Ltd., London, 1933.

  I've always enjoyed this book written by a practical and thorough craftsman. And I've always wanted to try his recipe for an "emergency" waterproofing cement, that is: "crumbling whitening into a tin of ready mixed black paint"—but somehow I've always chickened out.

  Great drawings and photographs.

  Written as a first book for the amateur, the author recommends Whall's STAINED GLASS WORK and Twining's THE ART AND CRAFT OF STAINED GLASS for those who want to extend their knowledge to painting on glass.

- Mollica, Peter, STAINED GLASS PRIMER VOLUMES 1 & 2, photography by Charles Frizzell, Vol. 1 edited by Norm Fogel, Mollica Stained Glass Press, Berkeley, Ca.
  Vol. 1: The Basic Skills, 1971.
  Vol. 2: Advanced Skills and *this* Annotated Bibliography, 1977

- Nervo, Joanne, STAINED GLASS PATTERNS, Nervo, Berkeley, 1972.
  Dedicated to a retired glass man, Albert Stagnaro, this book reprints hundreds of old designs from the catalogs of Victorian stained glass studios. It also has photographs of lampshades to give the reader ideas.

- Newton, Eileen, STAINED GLASS IS EASY, Theta Bookworks, Box 843, Willows, California 95988, 1977.
  Copper foil for the beginner.

- Reyntiens, Patrick, THE TECHNIQUE OF STAINED GLASS, Watson-Guptill Publishers, New York City, 1967.
  This book led the way for all the recent technique books. It is still among the best and most comprehensive. It covers Dalle-de-Verre, fused glass, epoxy glass on glass, as well as the traditional techniques of leaded glass. The section on painting on glass is thorough and offers methods of applying and manipulating the paint that go beyond the traditional techniques. Photographs of the many effects possible using expressionistic techniques to apply and texture the paint before firing.

My other favorite chapter is that which describes the ideal studio, from tea-making equipment to insurance. Although much of this advice is beyond the reach of most artists just starting out, the theory behind suggesting a separate room for each operation is sound. Having an ideal in mind can be very helpful when you go to make up your own studio. But don't get discouraged if you can't have it all at once.

Chapters proceed in a logical sequence as the steps in making a window: cutting, painting, firing, glazing, installing with additional sections on packing, exhibiting, and other techniques.

I understand that a revised and expanded edition is soon to appear.

- Rothenberg, Polly, CREATIVE STAINED GLASS, Crown Publishers, New York, 1973.

    Simple leaded glass instructions and also chapters on fused glass, slab glass, glass and epoxy, and paint on glass.

- Suffling, E.R., A TREATISE ON THE ART OF GLASS PAINTING, PREFACED WITH A REVIEW OF ANCIENT GLASS, Scott Greenwood and Son, London, 1902.

    Two color plates and thirty-six illustrations in the text.

    One of the only historians who sees the pinnacle of stained glass as the 15th and 16th centuries.

    I enjoyed the painting technique section very much, but my favorite things about this book are the illustrations on pages 88 and 127 of "glass painting brushes" and "glaziers tools" which I stole to reproduce in this book. My thanks to Ernest Suffling.

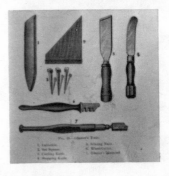

FIG. 4.—St. John (Tracery Piece).

- Twining, E.W., THE ART AND CRAFT OF STAINED GLASS, Sir Isaac Pitman and Sons, Ltd., 1928, London.

In his introduction, Mr. Twining says, "With the ultra-modern school in the several fine arts I am not in sympathy. There is too great a tendency to be merely eccentric. Fortunately, there is not very much of this sort of thing done in stained glass. . . ."

After a section on the differences in dress of bishops and knights of the various centuries, Twining develops a rather complex window through all the details, and I mean details, of its construction or, as I'm sure he'd prefer, creation.

Great drawings and illustrations and great reading. Ever wanted to know, in pounds, exactly how hard to press your glass cutter to 3/32" glass? Well, it's in here along with countless other gems and some good useful information, too. I'd suggest that you already know a bit about stained glass technique before you use this book—it could be just confusing for a beginner. You might want to compare his chapter on easels with the one in this book.

I love this book.

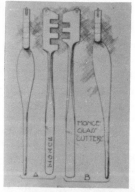
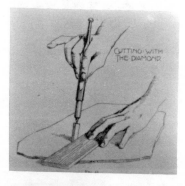

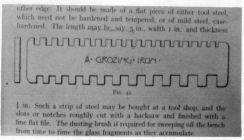

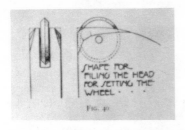

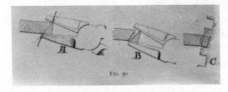

• Tysoe, Peter, GLASS, RESIN AND METAL CON-
STRUCTION, Mills and Boon, Ltd., London, 1971.
"Most of the work pictured in the illustrations is hideous,
but there may be valuable information of a technical nature
on the subjects of glass laminating and slab glass
construction."   —Ed Carpenter, 1977

- Vasari, Giorgio, VASARI ON TECHNIQUE, Dover Publications, New York, 1960. Translation by Louisa S. Maclehose, introduction and notes by Professor G. B. Brown.

This classic work was first published in 1550 in Italy. It is a description of the techniques involved in the architecture, sculpture and painting during the Renaissance. The section on painting contains a brief chapter on stained glass.

Vasari explains how a window is made and how enamels are used and finally, ". . . in order that boys and other nuisances should not spoil the windows, a fine network of copper-wire is placed behind them." The descriptions of the techniques are interesting but sketchy.

Professor Brown begins his notes on this chapter by admitting that stained glass ". . . is not a specially Italian form of the decorative art . . ." (I beg to differ.) He goes on to an interesting discussion of the enamels/no-enamels controversy, stating that the traditional no-enamel pot-metal window was favored north of the Alps while the 16th century Italian painter preferred a more delineated design painted on clear glass with enamels.

Professor Brown also gives a brief history of stained glass and enamelled glass. For a complete discussion of Italian stained glass see: Marchini, G., ITALIAN STAINED GLASS WINDOWS.

- Whall, C.W., STAINED GLASS WORK, Sir Isaac Pitman and Sons, Ltd., London, 1905.

As the editor says, this book is meant to be a ". . . trustworthy textbook of workshop practice."

And in a very workmanlike fashion, Mr. Whall sets out all the details of the craft of stained glass. He insists over and over that written instructions cannot teach good use of tools—it must be learned at the bench. And so his method of writing instruction is like speaking to his apprentice. And a very demanding master he would be.

He inserts many moral lessons for the student, like . . ."A note to be always industrious and work with all your might."

On grinding glass paint: "You must grind colour till it is smooth, and an old-fashioned *granite* muller is the thing, not a glass one." Well, now-a-days, a glass muller is old-fashioned so I'd better caution you that a *glass* muller is the thing, not a plastic one. Well, it's fun reading but in the end I think Mr. Whall has been too thorough for his written instruction to be easily followed. He offers "all three" alternative methods in ·a way that would, I think, be confusing to the student.

- Wood, Paul W., STAINED GLASS CRAFTING, Sterling Publishing Company, New York, 1967.
Brief technique instruction for leaded glass window, lamp, mosaic, faceted glass, glass on glass with epoxy, etc. And chapters on painting and firing glass, also some simple projects for schools. The last page has a good photograph of the huge glass mural on the American Airlines terminal at Kennedy Airport, New York City by Robert Sowers.

11 *Waste bin on wheels*

From Reyntiens, THE TECHNIQUE OF STAINED GLASS

3. Stained Glass: General

- Bachem, J.P., DAS HANDWERK IM DIENSTE DER KIRCHE, Verlag J. P. Bachem, Köln, 1955. Translated "Handwork in Service to the Church."

  Black and white photographs of objects made for churches, candle holders, book bindings, crosses, lecterns, and ten postwar windows from German designers.

- Baker, John, "Stained Glass Today" from the ARCHITECTS' YEAR BOOK 6, Elek Books Ltd., London, 1955.

  After a brief rundown on the history of stained glass Baker sums up the deplorable state of the art by saying, ". . . the only real difference between some present day stained glass artists and their 19th century counterparts lies in that the Victorians were a good deal more competent, not only in their drawing and design but also as craftsmen." What hope then, in 1955? Baker seems to think that new techniques are the key, but he ends on this note, "Not isolated panels in a wall drawing attention to themselves, but a wall of glass or combination of glass and wall surface, which contributes to rather than steals from the architectural setting. This can only come about by proper cooperation between the artist-designer and the architect, and between these two and glass manufacturers and technicians."

- Bayless, J.H., JEWELS OF LIGHT, Washington Cathedral, Washington, D.C., 1975.

  This booklet is available from the Washington Cathedral and it describes with color photographs and brief words the windows of the cathedral. An introductory section discusses stained glass in general and the cathedral's use of it . . . "those who guide the Cathedral's policy have sought to achieve the utmost in splendid color through careful adherence to the primary reds, blues and golds . . ."

- Brady, D. and Serban, W., STAINED GLASS, INFORMATION GUIDE SERIES ON ART, Gale Research Company, Detroit, 1977.

  In their own words: "The volume will mostly consist of bibliographic annotations on major English language works on stained glass as well as information regarding suppliers, publishers, artists, exhibitions, workshops and apprenticeships relating to the topic of stained glass. It is intended to appeal to a broad range of publics, particularly researchers and skilled craftspersons, but also hobbiests and the person interested in 'how-to-do-it'."

- Chagall, M., VITRAUX POUR JÉRUSALEM, Musée des Arts Décoratifs, Paris, 16 June - 30 September, 1961.

  Catalog of the Paris show of Chagall's windows before their installation in Jerusalem. Lots of photographs and French text.

- Connick, Chas. J., ADVENTURES IN LIGHT AND COLOR, George G. Harrap and Company, Ltd., London, 1937. Also Random House, New York City, 1937.

My favorite stained glass book. I like this book because it's not like all the other stained glass books. It's more personal and less a re-hash of earlier books. The same is true of Connick's windows. Connick said, "The supreme achievement in this world is not a painting nor a poem—great as they are—the supreme achievement is a life. And the art of living is the supreme art."

So his book talks as much about life and his life as it does about stained glass and his stained glass.

I'druther have glass the way God made it.

- Engels, Mathias, CAMPENDONK ALS GLAS-MALER, Scherpe Verlag, Krefeld, 1966, good photographs, German text.

  Campendonk was a student of Johan Thorn Prikker, so was Anton Wendling. Whereas Wendling built his style from the geometric abstractions of Thorn Prikker, Campendonk extended Thorn Prikker's figurative style and made it his own. His windows are complex and forceful with a very strong, active leadline which does not, however, stray far from the traditional function of surrounding shapes and denoting a change in color. There is some use of the leadline as the graphic "subject" of the designs, but not nearly so much as we see in Thorn Prikker or later in Schaffrath and Schreiter.

- Freund, M., JEWELS FOR A CROWN, McGraw-Hill Book Company, New York, 1962.

  Meant for young, gullible people, this book describes Marc Chagall's creation of the windows for the Hadassah Medical Center in Jerusalem.

The Chagall windows set in the synagogue "in the hills of Judea."

- Hill, Hill and Halberstadt, STAINED GLASS MUSIC FOR THE EYE, Scrimshaw Press, Oakland, California, 1976.

  This book starts by making the tired analogy between stained glass and a symphony—it never goes much deeper into the subject of stained glass than that. It proclaims how glorious stained glass was through its history and shows examples of 19th and 20th century windows. The selection of windows shown ranges from very good to very bad, but the photographs (all in color) are superb as is the quality of the production. Halberstadt has a tendency to show us close-ups of parts of windows rather than whole windows in their architectural settings. This makes a very beautiful book, but I would have liked to see the windows shown in their settings.

- Hoff, August, JOHAN THORN PRIKKER, Verlag Aurel Bongers, Recklinghausen, 1958.

  A small, hard-to-find book with short German text and some very good color and black and white photographs. For further comment on Thorn Prikker, see Wember, P., JOHAN THORN PRIKKER.

- Hofstätter, Hans, JOHANNES SCHREITER NEUE GLASBILDER, Heinz Moos Verlag, Munich, 1965, German text.

  Johannes Schreiter is very well known as a painter as well as a glass designer. He is one of the giants of Post World War II German glass design (See GLASS ART, August, 1975, p. 10). This book offers some excellent photographs of some of his work up to 1965—since then he has changed style considerably and it's time for another book. I think this style change is the most dramatic of all the Germans. His windows, as in this book, were very complex and active—almost violent in the amount of motion they suggested, but his newer designs are often quiet compositions of very few leadlines, or static rows of parallel leadlines with large still forms in quiet colors. Schreiter feels that his painting and stained glass design should parellel each other and change in one should be reflected in the other.

  A must!

- Kampf, Avram, CONTEMPORARY SYNAGOGUE ART, 1945-1965, Union of American Hebrew Congregations, New York City, 1966.

  Synagogues have been very open to using modern design in stained glass. This book contains examples, among them Adolph Gottlieb's windows for Steinberg House, New York City and several windows by Robert Sowers. Also included is the design for Ben Shahn's window in Temple Beth Zion, Buffalo, New York. The window itself is very beautiful, though difficult to photograph.

- Katholische Akademie Schwerte, BUSCHULTE, WILHELM, 5840 Schwerte/Ruhr, Bergerhof Weg 24, 1973, German text.

  This was a catalog for a show of the work of Wilhelm Buschulte, one of the leading stained glass designers in Germany. It contains seven black and white photographs of windows and a list of his windows, 1953-1973. This list is very valuable, but is not by any means complete as Buschulte has done much work since 1973 and his style has changed considerably from the work pictured here. He delights in the use of strong color which the photographs do not show.

  A full scale study and documentation of his work is called for, as no book now exists on his work, that I know of.

- Lammers, Egbert, GLASFENSTER VON EGBERT LAMMERS, Josef Keller Verlag, Starnberg, 1966.

  Black and white and color photographs—39 pages of work by Lammers. Short text in German.

  Most of Lammers' windows are figure subjects in a modern sort of expressionistic style.

- Leymarie, J., THE JERUSALEM WINDOWS, George Braziller, New York City, 1967.

  Photographs and descriptions of Chagall windows for the Hadassah-Hebrew University Medical Center.

- Lloyd, J.G., STAINED GLASS IN AMERICA, Foundation Books, Jenkintown, Pennsylvania, 1963. S.G.A.A.'s view of what was happening in 1963.

  A little history, a little technique, a chapter on how to purchase a stained glass window. Lots of photographs of windows done by member studios, including some of the worst I've ever seen.

  The couple of windows from Emil Frei studios, one in black and white and the other in color, stand out as very interesting design and a bit out of place in this book.

- Loire, Gabriel, THE CATHEDRAL OF CHARTRES, ITS INFLUENCE ON THE ART OF GLASS, Loire Imports, Inc., New York City.

  The alluring title of this book sets one up to be disappointed. It is merely a public relations publication of the Loire Stained Glass Studio which is located near the Cathedral of Chartres and likes to be identified with it.

  The best of Loire's windows are among the best slab-glass windows made, so far, in my opinion.

  This book shows some examples of his work, in black and white. I remember the window on p. 46 from South Hamilton, Massachusetts. It overwhelms with its size in the small church. I always liked it because it was a little more mysterious than most of the church windows I'd seen at that time. Now I think I would question if much of the mystery wasn't just the confusion of the shattered appearance that characterizes most slab glass. I would also question the appropriatenes of the overwhelming size and abundance of color in that small, gentle sanctuary. I hope I could still like the window some.

  The question implied in the title is a very interesting subject for an essay. One of Chartres' influences on Loire is that he ". . . never loses sight of the essential function of stained glass, intended to create an atmosphere of mysticism, and a spiritual climate that affects the soul and draws it closer to another world where material considerations disappear." The modern church does not always see things that way. Criticism from within and outside the church has made the image of the sheltered, withdrawn, separate-from-the-real-world church not always desirable.

Many churches are letting the real world enter the sanctuary and bathe the worshipper in the glorious light of community and responsibility. Whether that rules out the use of stained glass or merely the influence of Chartres is a question even more alluring.

- Oidtmann, 100 JAHRE RHEINISCHE GLAS-MALEREI, Verlag Gesellschaft Für Buchdruckerei Ag, Neuss, 1957.
  A very hard-to-find book chronicling the work of Oidtmann studios over the 100 years prior to 1957. Includes some photographs of windows from the 1950's designed by the great modern German artists.

- Oliphant, F.W., A PLEA FOR PAINTED GLASS, BEING AN INQUIRY INTO ITS NATURE, CHARACTER, AND OBJECTS, AND ITS CLAIMS AS AN ART, J. H. Parker, Oxford, 1855.
  This is only a 72 page book, but as you can tell from the title, Mr. Oliphant likes to pack his sentences full of words.

  Here is a book for those readers who have a compulsion to wade through everything ever put in print on the subject. Lesser souls will probably founder in the preface, if they haven't already done so in the title.

- Overy, Paul, DE STIJL, E. P. Dutton, New York, 1969.
  De Stijl means the style in Dutch. Theo von Doesburg named his magazine De Stijl and advocated a style which contributed greatly to the development of design in the 20th century. There is on p. 112 a photograph of a window van Doesburg designed in 1921. Its similarity in feeling to much of Thorn-Prikkers windows is startling and makes me wish that the history of that decade in Europe was better documented in English. None of the histories of stained glass ever even mention van Doesburg or, for that matter, Josef Albers or who knows how many others who experimented in stained glass between the wars.

- Pfaff, Dr. Konrad, LUDWIG SCHAFFRATH: STAINED GLASS AND MOSAIC, Forward by Erich Stephany, Scherpe Verlag, Krefeld, Germany, 1977. (Available in the USA from C & R Loo, Box 8473, Emeryville, Ca. 94662.) 160 pages and 180 illustrations, 24 in color.

  This book on one of the great stained glass designers of Germany is long overdue and should offer much for the young designers of this country.

  Inge Bartolome shows us Schaffrath's work in superb photographs.

  The text traces the development of the artist as he experiments in all media until, in the late 1950's, glass becomes the main material. Dr. Pfaff discusses the innovations and philosophy that made Schaffrath's work unique.

- Piper, John, STAINED GLASS: ART OR ANTI-ART, Studio Vista, London, 1968.

  John Piper is well known in England as a painter as well as part of the John Piper/Patrick Reyntiens team who created windows for many churches in England including Coventry and the Catholic Cathedral at Liverpool.

  His message in this book is, I think, that stained glass should be designed by artists. He means specifically painters, like Chagall, Leger, Manessier, Matisse and, of course, Piper.

He feels that professional stained glass designers have not done a good job. At the time, he was not, it appears, familiar with the modern German designers. Except for a 1926 quote from Herbert Read about Thorn-Prikker, D. Böhm's window wall at Maria Königin Church in Cologne, and Buschulte's windows in Maria Königin in Saarbrücken, he makes no mention of Germany.

What he wants is good stained glass and who can blame him. His selection of photographs is different from what you'll see in most stained glass books. My favorite is the exterior of a church window glazed in old clear glass and reflecting the trees in the yard (p. 43), with the very important caption, "Does this church really need more stained glass?"

• Quagliata, N., STAINED GLASS FROM MIND TO LIGHT, Mattole Press, San Francisco, 1976.

This book is subtitled: "An inquiry into the Nature of the Medium,"—I don't consider it that. For me, it is much more an inquiry into the author's approach to art. At a time when the market is flooded with how-to-do-it stained glass books, Quagliata wanted to give students some directions on how-to-design-it. I don't know if you can do that in a book—more likely you show them how—"I"—design-it. That can be valuable for the beginner.

One section of Quagliata's book discusses and shows students fabricating a single large panel for a public building. The students participated in all the processes of cartooning and making the window, experiences which they could never have gotten on their own.

As added inspiration for young designers, Quagliata presents, in his final chapter, the work for five of his contemporaries. Each artist shows photographs and gives an introductory statement about his/her work. This is a very valuable addition to this book.

- Rigan, Otto, NEW GLASS, San Francisco Book Company, 1976.

  NEW GLASS looks at twenty-four west coast stained glass artists and their work. It is the first book that presents work by younger artists who are treating stained glass in unconventional ways. The excellent photographs by Charlie Frizzell (who did all the photographs for STAINED GLASS PRIMER, Vols. 1 and 2) are the main content of the book. An introductory chapter by Otto Rigan gives an historical summary of the evolution of stained glass and calls the work documented an "omni-movement—without a declared manifesto, statement of purpose or restriction whatever." Some might call it a mish-mash of divergent styles. The rest of the book consists of a section for each of the twenty-four artists with an introduction by Otto Rigan followed by a statement by the artist. There are black and white photographs of each artist in his/her studio and of some of his/her work. The center section of the book contains sixty-four pages of color photographs of windows by the twenty-four artists.

  I think this is an important book. A must!

  Charlie says, "Buy this book immediately!"

- Soraci, C., THE CONVICT AND THE STAINED GLASS WINDOWS, Dell Publishing Company, Inc., 1961.

  How to win freedom from Sing Sing by switching from "paper hanging" to stained glass window making.

  This book is an autobiography of Carelo Soraci who grew up a forger and general bad hat, but found in prison that making stained glass windows was more fun than making license plates.

  Corny at times, but I liked it.

- Sowers, R., THE LOST ART, George Wittenborn, Inc., New York City, 1954.

  Sowers traces the art of stained glass through the height of its glory in Gothic Europe and follows it through its depths in the Renaissance, explaining what made it great and what contributed to its near disappearance.

  Most important are his discussion and photographs of how some modern trends could lead to great stained glass in the 20th century. He was right and he was the only voice that told us it was coming. Absolutely essential reading, though almost impossible to find.

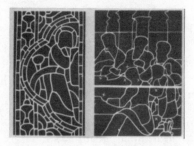

- Sowers, R., STAINED GLASS: AN ARCHITECTUR-
AL ART, Universe Books, New York City, 1965.

The most important stained glass book published in English. Out of print, although Universe Books could be cleaning up if they would just reprint it.

I find something new here every time I pick it up. The first time, in 1965, I was just overwhelmed by the photographs. I'd never seen windows like this before. As I confront new problems of designing windows for architecture I always find well thought out words of wisdom in it.

This book is about stained glass as art, most books deal with stained glass as archeology.

This is one of the very few books that approaches and analyzes stained glass from a point of view younger than the mid-1850's. In the twelve years since it was published it has remained the only book, in English, which discusses, in depth, the 20th century use of stained glass in architecture; how windows affect the buildings they are in and vice-versa. Sowers talks about what things are important to consider when designing for architecture. Sowers has been designing windows for twenty-five years or so. He offers us the benefit of his experience. His book also contains exceptional photographs of some of the best work from all over the world. If you're fed up with seeing nothing but Tiffany, or "The Disneyland Medievalists" windows, then you're in for a treat.

- Wember, Paul, JOHAN THORN PRIKKER, GLAS-FENSTER, WANDBILDER, ORNAMENTE, 1891-1932, Scherpe Verlag, Krefeld, 1966, text in German.

Many very good color photographs of Thorn Prikker's windows, mosaic, murals, textile design and paintings. Thorn Prikker was a contemporary of Toulouse-Lautrec, Matisse, and Peter Behrens. His first paintings as a member of the Dutch "Luminist" group are most like "pointillism" and two from 1896-7 are shown in this book. But after 1910 Thorn Prikker became very much interested in stained glass and by then his style was very different from those first paintings. He became very well known for his stained glass and was a major influence on the work of many other artists including Josef Albers, Heinrich Campendonk and Anton Wendling. Wendling and Albers both did stained glass that was inspired by Thorn Prikker. After World War II Wendling became Ludwig Schaffrath's teacher and many of the other modern German designers owe a great debt to Thorn Prikker. But he should not be appreciated only for his influence, his windows are still around and still great.

Perhaps his masterpiece is St. George in Cologne on which he was working when he died in 1932.

A must! An English translation of this book would be a great service.

- White, Norval, THE ARCHITECTURE BOOK, Alfred Knopf, New York, 1976.

  The words and people of architecture. A kind of brief encyclopedia on the subject. Lots of small, poor quality black and white photographs. Starts with Aalto and ends with Zoophorus.

  The stained glass entry says: "Modern stained glass was carried to extremes that made whole churches of it..." and gives Perret's 1923 church at La Raincy as an example.

  Want to know what a stanchion, a wythe, tufa, a stupa, or a Stubbins is? Then this is a book for you.

- Wingler, Hans, THE BAUHAUS, M.I.T. Press, Cambridge, Massachusetts, 1969.

  Page 330-331 deal specifically with the stained glass workshop at the Bauhaus in the early 1920's. It seems that the input of Itten, Klee and Albers, all of whom supervised its running, was not enough to keep it afloat. The tradition of church use made it difficult to find an application in the new architecture. The text has little more to offer; the photographs consist of two windows by Albers and a shot of the studio as it existed in 1923. There was no one working when the picture was taken, everything looked neat and clean.

- Yoki, MODERN SWISS STAINED GLASS, Office du Livre, 1971, text in French and German, twenty color and forty black and white photographs.

  These modern windows are not as powerful as the German stuff, but it's obvious that the Swiss have not been standing still or looking back like most other countries.

  The windows from the 1920's and 30's show the beginnings of new thought. This book covers such a wide variety of designers that the total effect is a bit scattered. I'd like to see more of a few of the designers and little or nothing of some of the others.

Magazines

- AMERICAN MAGAZINE OF ART, "William Willet and his Work in Stained Glass," The American Federation of Arts, Metropolitan Museum, New York, Volume 12, Number 9, September, 1921, pp. 314-317.

  This is an obituary for William Willet. It lists and lauds his major work and quotes two neo-Gothic architects praising his windows.

- ARCHITECTURE AND ENGLISH NEWS, "Stained Glass: Tradition Meets Technology," November, 1969.

  Photographs of Willet Fabrigem windows and others by Jacoby Studios, Duval Studios and two by Robert Frei, in my opinion, one of the few older studios whose designs really consider the architecture. Also pp. 30-45, article on plate glass for skyscrapers.

- ARTIFEX JOURNAL OF THE CRAFTS, Vol. 1, 1968, Oriel Press, London.

  Stained glass and blown glass in England; article on Whitefriar's studio archives mentioning Wiliam Morris, etc.

- THE ART GALLERY MAGAZINE, "Gaudí," Hollycroft Press, Ivoryton, Connecticut, Summer, 1975, pp. 42-47.

  A short article on architect, Antonio Gaudí. Several excellent color photographs of his buildings including one shot of his windows in the Casa Batlo, Barcelona. The article recommends a new book: GAUDÍ by Salvador Tarragó, published by Escudo de Oro, S. A., Palaudarias, 2G, Barcelona 4. I have not found it in English translation yet.

- CURRÂNT MAG; May-June-July, 1976, San Francisco, California, p. 49, 56-58.

  An interview with Claire Falkenstein who made the odd-looking window (pictured on p. 49) which is in St. Basil Church, Wilshire Boulevard, Los Angeles. Claire says in the interview that her windows for this church were part of the reason she "was given the Los Angeles Woman of the Year Award in Art in 1969."

- Carpenter, Ed, "Stained Glass in Germany and Britain," CRAFTS MAGAZINE, September, 1973, London.

  A Must. This very important interview is largely responsible for introducing the work of the modern German glass designers to Britain. When reprinted in April, 1975, it helped bring that awareness to America. Carpenter discusses the differences in the working methods of the German designers and explains why this has helped to develop "a sense of direction" in German glass design rather than the many dissimilar styles one sees in England and America. Carpenter, in looking to the future, calls for a greater awareness of architecture on the part of stained glass designers and looks forward to involvement with the architecture of business and industry.

- CREATIVE ART: A MAGAZINE OF FINE AND APPLIED ART, Vol. 2, Number 1, p. 29, New York, January, 1928.

  Page 29 of this issue shows a black and white photograph of the interior of a bank in Holland designed by H. F. Mertens. No mention is made in the accompanying article about the enormous leaded glass ceiling. I have never seen other mention of it and I doubt if it still exists—if you're going to The Hague, you might check if the bank of Rotterdam branch office has survived. The glass looks a lot like Thorn Prikker's design and The Hague was his birthplace.

- DAS MÜNSTER, 1961-1969, Verlag Schnell and Steiner.
The only source of photographs of stained glass being done in Germany since the war. During the 1960's they published about a dozen issues with outstanding stained glass. Unfortunately, it has tapered off in the 1970's and now hardly a window is published all year to justify the subscription rate. Oh well, all things must pass. Text in German with English summaries. A must.

- "Old Medium, New Messages," EBONY, December, 1971, pp. 33-42.
Article on the work of artist Douglas Phillips of Cleveland, Ohio.

- Eckhardt, Wolf von, "Through the Glass Brightly," HORIZON, Horizon Publishing Company, New York, September, 1962, pp. 22-32.
Short predictable text accompanies some good color photographs of windows by Bazaine, Chagall, Helmut Landir, Manessier, as well as a great photograph of Heinz Bienefeld's wall at Maria Königin Church in Cologne.

- FAITH AND FORM, JOURNAL OF THE GUILD FOR RELIGIOUS ARCHITECTURE, Published biannually at 177 Church Street, N.W., Washington, D.C. 20036.

Occasional photographs of stained glass, discussion of church architecture. Should be a better magazine if church architects begin thinking a bit more about what they build.

- FRANCE - ILLUSTRATION LE MOND, Noël, 1951, Numero 320.

Section on the windows of the "Chapelle du Rosaire des Dominicaines de Vence" by Henri Matisse.

Good color photographs of the windows and other Matisse designed appointments for the chapel.

- GLASS ART MAGAZINE, Portland, Oregon

1973, January/February: This first issue features eight windows by Paul Marioni accompanied by his descriptions.

June/July, Mangan, M., "Ludwig Schaffrath: Designing Stained Glass to Complement Architectural Exteriors," this article discusses Schaffrath's use of flashed opak glasses to make his windows read in shades of white and grey from the exterior of buildings. Six black and white photographs (printed in blue ink, unfortunately).

1974, February: Sowers, Robert, "Autonomous Panels," Seven black and white photographs.

April: Wilson, David, "Some Thoughts on Stained Glass Design," seven black and white photographs.

October: Reyntiens, P., "Ludwig Schaffrath; Show of Cartoons for Stained Glass," plus photographs of work by Clive Blewchamp, A. R. "Casey" Lewis, and Kathie Bunnell.

1975, February: Sowers, R., "Stained Glass in Germany," important article reprinted from May, 1969, CRAFT HORIZONS.

April: Many stained glass features including interview with Ed Carpenter; stained glass tour of Germany by L. Schaffrath; article on stained glass school at Swansea; work by Robert Sowers, David Wilson and Leifur Breidfjord.

May: Kahlmann, Robert, "The Stained Glass of William Morris;" and Kehlmann, Robert, "Peter Mollica: Leaded Glass Artist;" and an article on stained glass at Louisiana State University.

August: von Roenn, Ken, "Johannes Schreiter," article and lots of photographs of the work of Schreiter, a very great designer of stained glass.

October: most of the issue devoted to articles about the work of Ludwig Schaffrath, both stained glass and mosaic. A very important contribution.

December: articles on medieval stained glass including: Sowers, R., "Some Wayward Lessons from the 'Poor Man's Bible';" Marchini, G., "Conservation of Stained Glass in Italy;" Walls, D., "Restoring Glass at York."

The issues I've chosen to single out are of particular interest to me; my view is quite prejudiced and I would recommend a thorough study of GLASS ART MAGAZINE. Early issues may be hard to find, but try libraries and schools where glass blowing is taught.

My feelings about this magazine in general have run from wild enthusiasm and support to angry criticism and disappointment, but no matter what I think, GLASS ART MAGAZINE has been one of the only sources of communication for glass people. We should be very glad that the attempt was ever made by Albert Lewis, the publisher, and by the past STAINED GLASS editors, Dan Fenton and Robert Kehlmann.

- HOUSE BEAUTIFUL, January, 1956, pp. 40-48, "Our Strongest Influence for Enrichment."

  An article on the architecture of Frank Lloyd Wright. It contains some rarely published color photographs of some of his stained glass very similar to windows of the Scottish architect, Charles Rennie Macintosh done about the same time. There's no denying Wright's influence on everything he touched and so with stained glass.

- Lee, L., "Modern Secular Stained Glass," ARCHITECTURAL DESIGN, Vol. XXI, Number 5, London, May, 1951.

  I've never found a copy of this article, but it sounds promising.

- LITTON INDUSTRIES ANNUAL REPORT, 1967.

  Litton points out the parallels between stained glass windows and corporate image. If you weren't aware of the similarities you're in for surprise.

• Hildebrand, J.R.,"Glass Goes to Town," NATIONAL GEOGRAPHIC, January, 1943.

The glass industry in 1943. Photographs showing products and machines, even one color photograph of a stained glass window being painted at Connick studio. Also stacked cylinders at Blenko Glass Company.

• Pitz, H.D., "The Willet Studios," AMERICAN ARTIST, December, 1958, pp. 30-36, 62-63.

A little history of Willet studios and description of slab glass technique and Henry Willet's own gold leafed lead sheet technique which I'll not attempt to describe.

Lucien Clarret strokes a gold-leaf brush in his hair prior to flying leaf on the leaden form.

• PROGRESSIVE ARCHITECTURE, "Stained Glass: Art or Business," March, 1968.

Studios vs. independent designers; who produces the best windows? Are the studios in it just for the money? Should the artist do free preliminary design sketches just to get the job? Brings up some important questions and tries to give both sides a chance to answer in this brief, but very good article.

• Rowell, Margit, "On Albers' Color," ART FORUM MAGAZINE, January, 1972.

Josef Albers was involved with stained glass in his years at the Bauhaus and worked with sandblasted flash glass.

This article, by the author of a book on Albers, was very important for me because it gave historical insights about the little-written-about stained glass studio at the Bauhaus. There is also a most interesting section on Johan Thorn Prikker and his influence on Albers.

Before I began to find this type of historical connections, the Post-war German glass design seemed to have popped up from nowhere. It has aided my study greatly to begin to understand what went before.

- Schreiter, J., "Stained Glass Today," KUNST UND KIRCHE, Number 3, 1973, pp. 122-125, German text.
Schreiter is one of Germany's top stained glass designers and in this article he discusses why the church seems less interested in stained glass in the 1970's than it was in the 1960's.
He calls for a meditative, more introverted art.

- Seckler, D.G., "Adolph Gottlieb Makes a Facade," ART NEWS, March, 1955, pp. 42-45, 61-62.
Photographs and story of Gottlieb's window wall for the Milton Steinberg Building, New York City.
Some shots of Heinigke studio making the windows.
Sketches for rejected designs and why he rejected them are the most interesting part of the article.

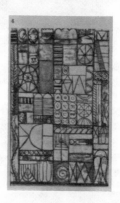

- SMITHSONIAN MAGAZINE: Frangiamore, C. L., "A Half-Century of Decorative Arts," Washington, D.C., May, 1973.
This article describes a show at the Renwick Gallery in Washington, D.C.: "The arts and crafts movement in America, 1876-1916." The article shows photographs of two F. L. Wright windows and one L. C. Tiffany window.

- Sowers, R., "New Stained Glass in Germany," CRAFT HORIZONS, May/June, 1969.

  A must! (Reprinted by GLASS ART, February, 1975)

  A very good introduction to the work of the German designers. Sowers' excellent writing helps clarify for us the important work done in Germany since the end of the war, how their designing is different from other stained glass design and the relationship of designer to studio.

- Sowers, R., "Thoughts on a Stained Glass Manual for Architects," CRAFT HORIZONS, November/December, 1960.

  Along with his fantasy of writing a primer on stained glass design, Sowers here gives us some good photographs of different style of architectural stained glass.

- SPACE DESIGN (SD), MONTHLY JOURNAL OF ART AND ARCHITECTURE, Number 34, September, 1967, Tokyo, Japan, pp. 103-105.

  Stained glass works by Jean Weinbaum. Five color plates and short Japanese text.

  Jean Weinbaum is a painter who has done some interesting stained glass.

- STAINED GLASS, Journal of the Stained Glass Association since 1903, St. Louis, Missouri.

  Chronicles the activities of the member studios producing church windows mostly in Neo-gothic styles.

  Interesting as history of an era of stained glass design that produced an immense volume of work. If you think that it was all bad then don't bother with the S G.A.A. Journal, cuz they thought it was good stuff.

  Their discussions of members' work seemed to consist only of flowerly praise or iconographical descriptions of the subject matter—never questioning whether or not it was good art. I guess they had to assume that all members had to be doing good art or they wouldn't be members.

  In the past couple of years, the magazine has broadened its outlook a bit and begun to take an interest in the new work being done in the U.S. and Europe. This is due to the openness of the current editor, Norman Temme, and the increased numbers of younger members attracted to the association.

- Willet, Anne Lee, "The Window," pp. 207-209, 223, ART AND ARCHEOLOGY, December, 1929.

  The glories of stained glass, the wickedness of 19th century opalescent picture windows and how William Willet single-handedly rescued us from this wickedness and turned us to the "glory that is glass."

  Anne Willet closes with this statement: "Only with our feet on the fundamentals of the media with which we work, putting behind our backs all hypocrises and shams, and pressing forward with honesty and reverence, will we be able to leave to posterity windows capable of transmitting uninterrupted rays of light which is the life of man. Remember Lot's wife."

- Willet, H.L., "Practical Considerations of Stained and Leaded Glass," ARCHITECTURAL FORUM, March, 1929.

  Meant for the instruction of architects, it discusses the materials used in a window as well as ventilator sash, method of installation, and how to commission a stained glass artist.

  I wonder if any architects found it interesting. Some must have, because H. L. Willet got lots of jobs over the years.

4. Glass: General

• Maloney, F. J. Terence, GLASS IN THE MODERN WORLD, Doubleday and Company, Inc., Garden City, New York, 1968.
Glass as a material, its properties, history and uses.
Good photographs and diagrams.
Glass is used for other things besides stained glass windows. If you didn't know that then this is a good book for you.

• Wilson, K., GLASS IN NEW ENGLAND, Old Sturbridge Village Booklet Series, Sturbridge, Massachusetts, 1959.
Booklet describes the history and techniques of early glass blowers in New England.
Photographs of Sandwich glass.

MAGAZINES

• American Crafts Council, Research and Education Department, 44 West 53rd Street, New York City 10019, BIBLIOGRAPHY: GLASS, 1975.
This bibliography will be useful to anyone looking for books on glass making and glass blowing. Has a section on stained glass which includes a list of CRAFT HORIZON articles on stained glass from 1954-1969.

• Brill, R.H., "Ancient Glass," SCIENTIFIC AMERICAN, Volume 209, Number 5, November, 1963.
Photographs of ancient glass vessels, photomicrographs of pieces of old glass, molecular arrangement drawings and interesting text about modern chemical and physical analysis of ancient Egyptian and Roman glass.

- Green, C.H., "Glass," SCIENTIFIC AMERICAN, Volume 204, Number 1, January, 1961.

  Interested in the atomic structure of glass? Its similarities to plastics? Is glass just an organic form of plastic?

  Does Corning glass works really develop thirty new glass formulas each day?

  C. H. Greene talks about all these and many more subjects like tempered glass, optical glass, glass fibers, sagging glass chunks to make telescope mirrors.

  Fascinating!

  P.S., p. 120 has a neat article on the growth of snow crystals.

- Smith, R.W., "History Revealed in Ancient Glass," NATIONAL GEOGRAPHIC, September, 1964, pp. 346-369.

  Ancient glassmaking . . . Rome, Egypt, etc.

- Adams, Henry, MONT-ST-MICHEL AND CHARTRES, 1904, Houghton-Mifflin and Company, Boston, 1936.

  A classic that is much more than a guide book to these famous cathedrals, although it serves that purpose very well.

  Through these two buildings Adams explores all the facets of the medieval mind, its philosophies and histories.

  "To feel the art of Mont-St-Michel and Chartres we have got to become Pilgrims again . . ." And as you prepare for your pilgrimage make this book part of your baggage.

- Aubert, M., LA CATHÉDRALE DE CHARTRES, Arthaud.

  Many photographs of the sculpture and a history of the cathedral in French.

- Batsford, H. and Fry, C., THE CATHEDRALS OF ENGLAND, B. T. Batsford, Ltd., London, 1934.

  Black and white photographs and descriptions of the cathedrals. Made as a kind of tour guide.

- Bottineau, Yves, NOTRE DAME DE PARIS ET ST. CHAPELLE, Rand McNally and Company, 1965.

  Four not-so-good color photographs of windows.

  A history and description of these two churches. Ideal as a preparation for a visit.

- Branner, Robert, Editor, CHARTRES CATHEDRAL, W. W. Norton and Company, 1969.

  A bunch of essays on Chartres, including translations of medieval documents and letters, two 17th century short histories of Chartres, and modern or semi-modern essays on the architecture, the sculpture and the stained glass.

  In "The Splendor of the Windows," by Maurice Denis, 1927, he says, "and it is not a useless lesson, in a complex era such as our own, to remind artists that one of the essential characteristics of art is naturalness and spontaneity."

  The other essay on stained glass is taken from H. Adams' MONT-ST-MICHEL AND CHARTRES.

194

- Clark, Kenneth, CIVILIZATION, Harper and Row, New York City, 1969.

  Kenneth Clark's chapter on "The Great Thaw" of the 12th century and his accounts of Abbot Suger and the beginnings of Gothic architecture and Chartres with her 170 windows is a very good introduction to what was going on at the time of Chartres.

- Gieselmann, Reinhard and Aebli, Werner, KIRCHENBAU, Verlag Girsberger, Zürich, 1959, text in German with a ten-page English summary and English captions.

  This book presents the thesis that church architecture has been in decline since the beginning of the 1800's. Traces the current of church building since the Middle Ages until it becomes no longer the leading architectural form, but is replaced by industrial architecture in the early 19th century. It then traces the attempts at a regeneration using examples from all over the world.

- Gimpel, John, THE CATHEDRAL BUILDERS, Grove Press, New York, 1971.

  The underground foundation structure of some of the cathedrals formed a stone mass as large as that above ground. You could build a fourteen-story building inside Beauvais Cathedral. All the sculpture on the façade at St. Denis was once painted in strong color. Legend says that where Notre Dame de Chartres now stands a grotto existed 100 years before Christ's birth. In that grotto a child-bearing virgin was worshipped. Medieval workmen worked a five-day week, often less.

  What other similarities are there between the 12th and 13th centuries and the 19th and 20th centuries? Fascinating stuff about the building of the cathedrals. There's a lot of information gathered here, but there would be very little come down to us if the workers weren't paid money which necessitated the keeping of accounts.

- Grodecki, L., CHARTRES, Draeger et Verve Éditeurs, Paris, 1963, French text.

  The monumental book on *the* monumental cathedral. Very wonderful and huge color photographs of Chartres, its windows and sculpture. Your snapshots cannot compare to these exquisitely detailed photographs. It's not like being there, but it's closer than anything I've seen. It would make a fantastic show—perhaps with even larger blow-ups of the photographs.

  Maybe that's not good—maybe it's better to leave Chartres as an experience only acquired through pilgrimage. No book or photographs could ever prepare one for the impact of first walking into Chartres.

- Grodecki, L., THE STAINED GLASS OF FRENCH CHURCHES, Linsay Drummand, Ltd., London, 1948, thirty-two color plates.

  History and good black and white photographs of cathedral interiors. Thirty-two color plates of close-ups of medieval stained glass.

- Harvey, John, THE MASTER BUILDERS, McGraw-Hill, New York, 1971.

  Who were the architects of the medieval cathedrals? Surprisingly, many are known and a few of their original drawings still exist. This book offers some good black and white and color photographs of medieval buildings that are not published as often as Chartres or Canterbury.

- Heer, F., THE MEDIEVAL WORLD: EUROPE 1100-1350, World Publishing Company, 1963.

  The power of the church and the aristocracy in medieval Europe. The Crusades and the intellectuals, background history to the study of medieval art.

  Lots of black and white photographs but not much stained glass.

- Henderson, G., GOTHIC, Penguin Books Ltd., Baltimore, Maryland, 1967.

  Twelfth and 16th century European art discussed, much of it relating to the cathedrals and to stained glass.

  Lots of good black and white photographs, but only a few of stained glass.

- Houvet, Etienne, CHARTRES CATHEDRAL, Helio-Lorraine, 1971.
  Another booklet available at the cathedral, this one revised by Malcolm Miller, the English guide of the cathedral.
  A history of the cathedral with descriptions of its art works.

- Houvet, E., MONOGRAPHIE DE LA CATHÉDRALE DE CHARTRES, Extrait d'un ouvrage couronné par l'Academie des Beaux-Arts.
  Lots of black and white and color. But my copy is unbound and I've never seen another so I don't know if it was ever published commercially.

- Jantzen, Hans, HIGH GOTHIC, Minerva Press, 1962.
  The 13th century, when Gothic architecture reached its finest hour, created the cathedrals of Chartres, Reims and Amiens. This book studies those three in detail. It compares the naves, choirs, the transepts, the sculpture and the stained glass.
  He deals with the stained glass briefly and mostly in terms of subject matter with some notes on the predominating color of various groups of windows.

- Macaulay, David, CATHEDRAL: THE STORY OF ITS CONSTRUCTION, Houghton Mifflin Company, Boston, 1973.
  Beautiful drawings and a great simplified story of the building of a cathedral as the workers joined their particular skills with those of other workers until the job was complete eighty-six years later.

- MacLeish, K., LEGACY FROM THE AGE OF FAITH, CHARTRES, National Geographic, December, 1969, pp. 856-882.
  Great photographs, romantic words, and good information on Chartres, the town, the cathedral and the windows.

- Malé, Emile, THE GOTHIC IMAGE, Harper and Brothers, New York, 1958.
  A study of religious art of 13th century France. More background on medieval artists.

- von Simson, Otto, THE GOTHIC CATHEDRAL, Pantheon Books, New York, 1956.
  What did the cathedral mean to the medieval builder and worshipper? Did they see what we see in it?
  In this book von Simson focuses on St. Denis and Chartres. He describes the book as an analysis of the architecture and says he only discusses the stained glass windows inasmuch as they belong to the architectural system.
  He says, "Notre Dame de Chartres is an edifice without architectural ornament. The architect designed his system with an eye to the great stained glass windows whose color and light would counterbalance the simplicity of his architecture."
  This book is one of the most interesting I've read about Chartres.

- Swaan, Wim, THE GOTHIC CATHEDRAL, Doubleday and Company, Garden City, New York, 1969.
  Lots of photographs, about 400. They saved the full page color for stained glass. Thirty-three different churches are presented from six countries.
  The book begins with essays on the times, the gothic style and building methods. A book for looking and if you've seen the buildings, to help you remember.

- Temko, Allan, NOTRE DAME OF PARIS, Time, Inc., New York, 1952.

  History of the cathedral of Notre Dame de Paris since the time when Parisiens worshipped pagan gods on her site.

  This book is obviously the result of a thorough study and gives insight not only into the church, but also into the people and their lives in medieval Paris.

  In the tradition of Henry Adams' MONT-ST-MICHEL AND CHARTRES, 1903, this book is based on love more than on science—nothing wrong with that.

- Villette, Jean, CHARTRES AND ITS CATHEDRAL, Artaud, 1963.

  History of cathedral and town with lots of good black and white photographs.

MAGAZINES

- "Chartres Cathedral," LIFE, December 15, 1961, pp. 52-71.

  Good photographs of cathedral and fair photographs of some of its windows.

- "Mosaics in Ravenna, LIFE, December 21, 1959, pp. 42-57.

  A bit of history and some excellent photographs of the mosaics.

6. Architecture: General

• Christ-Janer, Albert and Foley, Mary Mix, MODERN CHURCH ARCHITECTURE, McGraw-Hill, New York, 1962.

Forty Christian churches, monasteries and seminaries are presented with photographs, descriptions and architects' drawings. The text discusses the program for each church and the architect's response to the design problems. A lot has happened since this book was published, but the examples are good and it serves as an introduction. Perhaps an update is forthcoming.

• Cook, J. and Klotz, H., CONVERSATIONS WITH ARCHITECTS, Praeger Publishers, New York, 1973.

You might wonder what the most powerful architects of the 1960's were thinking about. Well, here they are in conversation, or nine of them at least. These men, and Denise Brown, all have many disciples who are out there building right now. Knowing how these nine think will help you enjoy and perhaps work with the architecture of the 1970's and 1980's.

• Damaz, Paul, ART IN EUROPEAN ARCHITEC-TURE, Reinhold Publishing Corporation, New York, 1956.

The frontispiece and cover photographs are details from the window wall by Heinz Bienfeld in St. Mary the Queen in Cologne. There are numerous photographs of stained glass and a great one of Matisse sitting in front of his windows at Vence. Also on p. 29 is a photograph of Josef Albers 1922 windows for Gropius' Sommerfeld House in Berlin. These windows came from Albers' association with the stained glass studio at the Bauhaus. Another great photograph is facing p. 84. It shows Georg Meistermann smoking a cigar in front of his 1952 window for the Broadcasting House in Cologne. Two other works by Meistermann are on pp. 169 and 173.

The text (pp. 62-67) on stained glass starts out by heralding the "surprising renaissance today" (1956). It seems everyone who has written about stained glass since 1750 has noticed a renaissance just starting. The author does not go much deeper into the subject and the high point of his text is when he calls for "a close collaboration between architect and artist."

Much of the art in architecture pictured here has that curious "modernistic" look to it which designed art seemed to have in the 1950's. A very interesting book all together. It's time for Damaz to do an updated version. If he doesn't, why don't you?

- Korn, Arthur, GLASS IN MODERN ARCHITEC-TURE, English edition, Barrie and Rockliff, London, 1967, originally published in German in 1929.

Written when glass was just coming into its own as a primary building material, this book gives pictures of the early buildings and projects of Mies Van der Rohe, Walter Gropius, Le Corbusier, as well as Arthur Korn. The photographs bear out the premise which he sets down in his introduction: ". . . it is now possible to have an independent wall of glass, a skin of glass around a building; no longer a solid wall with windows. . . . This window is the wall itself, or in other words, this wall is itself the window."

Well, whichever it is, it's meant a need for radical change in the thinking of stained glass designers. Even though Korn wasn't thinking about stained glass, this book has a lot to tell us.

- Mazmanian, Arthur B., THE STRUCTURE OF PRAISE, Barre Publishers, Barre, Massachusetts, 1973.

This is primarily a picture book of church architecture in New England. It has black and white photographs of many of the famous old church buildings and some very exciting pictures of some modern churches. In talking about some of the surprising forms of the new churches the author says, "Contemporary forms have not been inspired by flights of fancy, or a desire to revive the glories of past civilizations. They have been a serious, direct answer to the needs of contemporary society." (p. 76) And he quotes Paul Tillich, "The request that new building be stylistically contemporary is rooted in the nature of creativity and in the ethical principle of honesty."

- McGrath, Raymond, GLASS IN ARCHITECTURE AND DECORATION, The Architectural Press, London, 1937 (Revised, 1961).

"An encyclopedic book covering glass manufacture, glass in architecture and decoration, the nature and properties of glass and the glazing and fixing of glass into buildings. Full of fascinating photographs and diagrams in each chapter. Excellent coverage of landmark glass architecture such as the Crystal Palace. Stained glass section is sketchy to say the least. Photographs are a mediocre sampling of pre-1960's historical mish-mash.

"(p. 476) One very useful bit of information: Pilkington's discovery while consulting for a jam making factory that glazing the entire plant with yellow glass had the effect of ridding the place forever of flies—a possible sales pitch for stained glass (yellow) in kitchens, outhouses, pig sties?"— Ed Carpenter

- Pilkington Brothers, WINDOWS AND ENVIRONMENT, Pilkington Brothers, Ltd., 1969.

"Interesting summary of history of windows in architecture, their social and practical purposes, etc., but mostly technical information geared for architects designing illumination of their structures by natural light."—Ed Carpenter

- Porter, Tom and Mikellides, Byron, COLOR FOR ARCHITECTURE, van Nostrand Reinhold Company, New York, 1976.

Color for architecture seems to mean calling in the artist to help design buildings, which makes this a very pertinent book for stained glass designers.

The general tone of this book is that there is not enough color in our environment and that there should be more. In a sense they are right, but we do get large doses of color in cities and on highways via advertisements—we could perhaps do with a little less of this type of chaotic and insistent color bombardment. What we really need, or at least some of us, is a more organized presentation of color in rational doses. Ah-Ha. The "architectural" use of color—not "autonomous" (and representational) billboards of posters, subway stations, but entire walls painted red, instead. Well, this book gives much to think about and the photographs are interesting examples of color on buildings.

Since the book is about color, I have to comment on the unfortunate, but well-meaning, use of color photographs on black pages. The rationale was, I'm sure, that this would make the colors jump out of the page and look better, and it works with one color photograph in the middle of a black page, but with four or five different photographs squeezed onto each black page, it makes a very busy and distracting visual effect. White background would have been just the relief needed so that the eye could rest on each photograph without being distracted by the others. That's why it's usually done that way. Graphic designers are smart. Since Tom Porter is a teacher of graphics and design at Oxford Polytechnic, he should be smart like that. That's beside the point, it doesn't ruin the book. It's a good book, I think, and worth the price (I got it in a 40% off sale) just for the cover photograph of Gene Davis painting his stripes on the parkway approach to the Philadelphia Museum of Art.

• Scheerbart, Paul, GLASS ARCHITECTURE and Taut, Bruno, ALPINE ARCHITECTURE, Praeger, New York, 1972.

Both these works were written just after World War I. They have been called prophetic of the steel and glass architecture of the international style, but what these guys were really talking about was stained glass.

Scheerbart was a poet and he created a bunch of catchy mottoes to help spread the word, for instance: "coloured glass destroys hatred," "coloured happiness only comes in a glass culture," and my new favorite, "glass makes everything light so use it on the site." His buddy, Bruno Taut, was the architect and designed a glass pavilion for the German Werkbund Exhibition in Cologne in 1914. In the introduction, Dennis Sharp writes that the pavilion was an early prototype of the psychedelic pavilions now commonly seen at international exhibitions. Glass was everywhere: walls, ceilings, floors, stairs.

GLASS ARCHITECTURE consists of 111 short chapters, each praising the uses of glass and prophesying about how it will be when glass is king. He warns against "Tiffany effects in inartistic hands" and "figure representation in architecture" "when glass architecture gets in, there will not be much more talk of windows either, the word window will disappear from the dictionaries." "Not more light!—more coloured light!" And finally, "when home life has reached the stage where even the wildest fancies appear to be realized, the longing for something different ceases; people will travel only to learn about a particular type of glass art and possibly to bring it home—to be able to reproduce it in similar design."

- Schnell, Dr. Hugo, MODERN CHURCHES IN GERMANY, Verlag Schnell and Steiner, Munich, 1964.

This small pamphlet documents the "Eucharistic World Congress Exhibition of German Church Building and Art Since World War II" shown in Munich in 1960 and in Bombay in 1964. The buildings were represented in photographs and drawings, but evidently forty stained glass windows were sent as part of the display. This booklet has photographs of eighteen of them, including some early work by Meisterman, Buschulte, Schaffrath, Schreiter, Wendling, Katzgrau, Weigmann, and Poensgen.

- Schnell, Hugo, TWENTIETH CENTURY CHURCH ARCHITECTURE IN GERMANY, Verlag Schnell and Steiner, Munich, 1974.

This book ends with some color photographs of stained glass. It documents the history of German church architecture in time periods of: Before 1918; 1918-1945; 1945-1960; and after 1960.

Starting off with a decree of the Cardinal of Cologne, in 1912, that new churches are to be built in Romanesque or Gothic styles. In 1917, Otto Bartning wrote of these churches: ". . . Neo-Gothic and Neo-Romanesque trappings concealed the profane face of the preaching hall behind a lying facade of sacred symbolism, . . ." So began the fight that was to bring about a new alliance between art and church building. This history is detailed and meaty. It deals with the major figures and explains their influences showing plans and photographs of the churches.

Not much direct mention is made of the stained glass, but the main value of the book to stained glass artists is to explain the conditions which brought about the great work of the 1960's. A must!

- Schutte, Thomas F., Editor, THE UNEASY COALITION: DESIGN IN CORPORATE AMERICA: THE TIFFANY-WHARTON LECTURES, University of Pennsylvania Press, Philadelphia, 1975.

  A collection of essays by the likes of Louis I. Kahn, Thomas Watson and other biggies from the world of business and design. Good design may give you pleasure, but to these guys it means public relations and increased profits.

  "Design is a means toward accomplishing the end goals of serving markets and generating profits." (Intro, p. xiii)

  A call for an American Bauhaus: "The way things look is not irrelevant to the way things work: How they work is how they should look." (Ibid.)

  Educating executives is good but it must get into the school system for the people to demand good design—then you won't have to educate the executive when he's thirty cuz he'll have been exposed to it all his life. So not business schools, but grammar schools should be the target.

- Schwarz, Rudolf, THE CHURCH INCARNATE, THE SACRED FUNCTION OF CHRISTIAN ARCHECTURE, Henry Regnery Company, Chicago, 1958, Translated by Cynthia Harris; Originally published in German, 1938.

  Mies van der Rohe, in his forward to this edition, calls Rudolf Schwarz the Great German Church Builder and says that it is a difficult but great book.

  I agree that it is difficult reading and I'm not sure yet if it's a "great" book, but Rodolf Schwarz built some great churches. Modern stained glass and other art is an important part of his buildings and in this book he tells us what was going on in his head as he designed them.

- Sharp, Dennis, A VISUAL HISTORY OF 20th CENTURY ARCHITECTURE, New York Graphic Society, Ltd., Greenwich, Connecticut, 1972.

  A picture history of 20th century building, decade by decade. Sharp opens his introduction with this quote from Henry-Russell Hitchcock: "It is the forms, the shapes and the patterns of architecture which everyone first apprehends and which also have survival value." That's what you can see in this book—the shapes.

ACKNOWLEDGEMENTS

For their help in making this book possible, my thanks to: Lynn Barretti, Mary Ann Beach, California College of Arts and Crafts, Ed Carpenter, Dan Fenton, Norm Fogel, Chris Forester, Anne Fuller (Creative Arts Printing), Maestro Gaxiola, Brenda Hunt, Casey Lewis, Andy Magdanz, Paul Marioni, Margo Marsh, Ann McAndrew, George McKeever, Tony Mercurio (Mercurio Bros. Printing), Jennie Mollica, Judy Mollica, Beverly Reiser, L. Reusche & Co., Chris Rufo, Rich Samsel, Jeanne Stitt, Trinity Tool Co., Maria Vella, Victoria and Albert Museum, Western McArthur Co. Hope I didn't forget anyone.

The arrangement by decades, giving two to four pages to each year gives a very clear vantage point for viewing the parade of architecture since 1900. Each year has a few examples of buildings and a brief text. My two favorite photographs are both of brick buildings, p. 37, Hans Poelzig's 1912 chemical factory in Poland and p. 76, Peter Behrens' 1925 I G Farben A G in Frankfurt, Germany.

- Smith, G. E. Kidder, THE NEW CHURCHES OF EUROPE, Holt, Rinehart and Winston, New York, 1964.
  Sixty churches from twelve countries: photographs and a brief text for each building. A very interesting feature of this book is the printing on two fold-out pages of comparative plans, all to the same scale, for all sixty churches as well as photographs of each church interior looking toward the altar from just inside the entry. A very valuable book and it makes me wish that Mr. Smith would go back out there with his camera and do a follow-up.

- Weyres, Willy and Bartning, Otto, KIRCHEN, Verlag Georg D. W. Callwey, Munich, 1959, text in German.
  Hundreds of photographs and plan drawings for German churches. Only a slight indication of the great stained glass which was to become so prominent a part of German churches in the next decade.